Does the Internet Increase the Risk of Crime?

Other books in the At Issue series:

At ✸ Issue

Does the Internet Increase the Risk of Crime?

Lisa Yount, *Book Editor*

Bruce Glassman, *Vice President*
Bonnie Szumski, *Publisher*
Helen Cothran, *Managing Editor*

GREENHAVEN PRESS
An imprint of Thomson Gale, a part of The Thomson Corporation

THOMSON
™
GALE

Detroit • New York • San Francisco • San Diego • New Haven, Conn.
Waterville, Maine • London • Munich

THOMSON

GALE

LIBRARY OF CONGRESS CATALOGING-IN-PUBLICATION DATA

Does the Internet increase the risk of crime? / Lisa Yount, book editor.
   p. cm. — (At issue)
Includes bibliographical references and index.
ISBN 0-7377-2707-1 (lib. : alk. paper) — ISBN 0-7377-2708-X (pbk. : alk. paper)
  1. Computer crimes. 2. Internet. I. Yount, Lisa. II. At issue (San Diego, Calif.)
HV6773.D64 2006
364.16'8—dc22
                                           2005040257

Printed in the United States of America

Contents

Introduction

Even to those who use it fairly often, the Internet can seem like a dark, pathless forest. It is full of cryptic abbreviations and mysterious terms such as *proxy* and *secure socket layer.* An ever-growing number of books and articles, furthermore, warn computer users that dangerous creatures lurk in the Internet jungle. These predators use activities with harmless-sounding names like *spoofing* and *phishing* to perpetrate serious crimes, including identity theft, cyberstalking, and even cyberterrorism. Because these crimes employ or target computers, which many people find hard to understand, users often feel nearly helpless against them. However, users can go far to protect themselves against computer crime by following the kind of advice that most people heard in childhood.

Do Not Talk to Strangers

One of the Internet's greatest benefits is the fact that it allows easy communication among people anywhere in the world. However, the anonymity of the Internet also gives criminals the opportunity to conceal their real identity and to defraud and harm people. According to some experts, the warning not to talk to strangers is perhaps the most important advice in protecting oneself against computer crimes. Children are perhaps most at risk from computer communication because they have often not learned to be cautious. Wise parents will warn their youngsters not to give out their real names, addresses, or other personal information when talking on the Internet with people they do not know. Security experts emphasize, however, that the warning applies to adults, too. "The most obvious source of your information is you," writes TechTV's online scam expert, Becky Worley. Criminals gather and steal personal information to commit identity theft—fraudulently using this information to obtain credit, goods, and services. Most security specialists say that the best way to protect against identity theft, whether online or off, is not to give out vital information such as social security or credit card numbers unless absolutely necessary.

Beware of False Friends

Computers allow criminals to masquerade as trusted acquaintances or even friends. They may spread computer viruses by hijacking a computer and sending messages purporting to be from that computer's owner to everyone in the infected computer's e-mail address book. Because of this possibility, even e-mail attachments supposedly sent by friends should be regarded with suspicion if they are unexpected or sent with a nonspecific subject line such as "Check this out." Security specialists urge people not to open attachments in e-mail or download programs unless they are completely sure that these attachments or programs come from a safe source. They also advise users to install antivirus software and keep it up to date so that it will recognize newly developed viruses. "If you're connected to the Internet, you need antiviral software," states Reid Goldsborough, syndicated columnist and author of *Straight Talk About the Information Superhighway*, in a 2002 article in *Poptronics*.

In another kind of masquerade scam, identity thieves send e-mails claiming to come from a well-known company such as eBay or PayPal, requesting account information and including a link to what appears to be the company's Web site. The Web site looks almost exactly like the company's real one, but it actually belongs to a criminal. When people click on the link and enter information such as bank account numbers on the site, it goes directly into an identity or credit card thief's database. Because of such fake–Web site scams, called spoofing, banks, eBay, and other companies tell users that they will never request account information by e-mail. These businesses also recommend that users only contact them by directly typing in the company's Web address, or URL, rather than by clicking on a link in an e-mail.

Sometimes offline trickery helps people commit computer crimes. Former computer hacker Kevin D. Mitnick, now a security consultant, says that hackers often obtain passwords or other data they need to break into business systems by using what the hacker community calls social engineering. In his book *The Art of Deception: Controlling the Human Element of Security*, Mitnick provides many examples of how he and other hackers pretended to be fellow employees or other trusted insiders and simply asked people in companies for the information they wanted to know. The employees, seeing no harm in the requests, usually obliged. "You can buy the best [security] technology in the world and it won't protect [your] organization against social engineering," Mitnick told a reporter from the British publication *Information Age*. Mitnick and other security experts advise companies to train their employees to question even the most seemingly innocent requests.

Do Not Believe Everything You Hear (or See)

Using common sense to evaluate information, especially in an unsolicited e-mail ("spam"), can eliminate a lot of problems, say criminal investigators. How likely is it that someone will have inherited a fortune from a relative that they have never heard of, or that a Nigerian prince has chosen them out of the entire world's population to help in a secret transfer of money? How can a bank threaten to cut off the account of a user who never opened one? People need to be alert to ruses that ultimately aim to get them to share personal information.

Computer users should also be suspicious of deals that sound too good to be true. Most people are wary of buying supposed brand name watches or other "designer products" from someone selling them on the street, especially if the seller offers the merchandise for a tiny fraction of what it would cost in legitimate stores. Similarly, the chances of ultracheap products having the quality their Internet sellers claim are slim.

Lock Your Doors and Hide Your Keys

Just as locks and keys are needed to protect a house, security devices are needed to protect computers. One equivalent of a door lock in a computer is a firewall, software (and sometimes hardware) that monitors Internet transmissions to keep hackers and other unauthorized users out of a computer or a network. Reid Goldsborough and other experts agree that firewalls are just as important as antivirus software.

Most people know not to give out copies of their house keys or leave the keys where others might copy them. Police often recommend putting car keys and house keys on separate rings, for instance, so that if car keys must be left at a repair shop, the shop's employees will not be able to copy the house keys during the visit. Passwords are the keys to homes in cyberspace, and they must be chosen and guarded just as carefully as physical keys are. Security consultants warn computer users to make sure that no one can see them when they type in passwords in a public location such as a library or cybercafe. Indeed, they should not enter passwords for sensitive accounts such as bank accounts in public computers at all if they can avoid it because hackers can place programs in these computers that record users' keystrokes. In homes or offices, if people must write down passwords in order to remember them, they should do something less obvious with the notes than stick them on the computer monitor.

Computer crime experts like Becky Worley say that users should not make passwords from common words or from easily available personal information. "Your child's name, your birth date, or any information that lives in your permanent record is not a good password," she writes. If a user believes that someone may have learned a password to an important account, the password should be changed immediately, just like a house's keys and locks following a burglary. Worley and others recommend that people change their passwords often even if they have no reason to think that the passwords have been compromised. "In the end, your awareness of the danger of identity theft is your best defense," Worley says. Her advice can also help people protect themselves from other Internet crimes such as virus attacks and spoofing. Applying common sense and age-old warnings can greatly reduce the risk of being victimized and can guide users safely through the wilderness of the Internet.

1

Internet Crime Is Increasing

Chris Hale

Chris Hale is the former webmaster for the Criminal Justice Center at Sam Houston State University in Huntsville, Texas.

Cybercrime is an enormous international problem, yet national and global authorities cannot even agree on what it is, let alone how to fight it. One definition of cybercrime is illegal or illicit activities mediated by computers. Cybercrime can be divided into two main classes of offenses: those in which the computer is a target (such as hacking and computer sabotage) and those in which the computer is a means of committing the crime (such as cyberstalking, online fraud, and online distribution of child pornography). The cost and extent of cybercrime have been growing as Internet use rises around the world, and this growth is certain to continue. For a variety of reasons, law enforcement efforts have failed to keep up with cybercrime's expansion.

Following the terrorist attacks on September 11, 2001, a terrorist at a large European airport hacked into the airline's curbside check-in service and successfully provided clearance for him and 10 others to board flights to the United States under assumed names. In another incident, at a public library in a small Midwestern American town, a terrorist successfully hacked into the nation's computer network of hospitals and altered several medical records. This resulted in countless doctor errors and patient deaths. In still another incident, a hacker in

Russia created a computer virus that instructed oil tankers to capsize, resulting in huge financial loss and environmental catastrophe. Although the above scenarios are completely fictional, several cybercrime experts agree that occurrences such as these are highly plausible. According to a report by the National Research Council, "tomorrow's terrorist may be able to do more damage with a keyboard than with a bomb." In fact, [2002] estimates indicate that the Pentagon's computer networks are hacked into at least 250,000 times a year. Only 10% of all those penetrating government computers are ever caught and less than 6% actually result in a conviction. The U.S. Department of Defense also indicates that there are 13 known countries with information warfare or cyberterrorist programs directed against the United States. During the Kosovo conflict of 1999, Belgrade hackers declared cyberwar on NATO and successfully shut down all targeted servers. In December of 1995, an organization known as the Strano network launched a successful Internet strike against various French government websites, rendering them completely inoperable for 60 minutes. All of the above occurrences are forms of information warfare (IW) or cyberterrorism. Information warfare is defined as coordinated, systematic attacks against a nation's government and/or infrastructure through computers, communication systems and/or the media. Information warfare is only one of several types of cybercrime, thus a detailed discussion of IW is clearly beyond the scope of this article. Instead, this article intends to provide a broad overview of all aspects of cybercrime.

What Is Cybercrime?

Cybercrime is truly an international problem that affects all aspects of human life. Nonetheless, there is widespread disagreement, both nationally and globally, concerning an accepted definition of cybercrime. This is due in large part to the fact that cybercrime encompasses a wide range of offenses. For clarification purposes, most experts agree that cybercrime falls into one of three categories. First, a computer may be the target of criminal activity. This includes cases where an offender unlawfully breaks into a computer or computer system in order to damage the system or commit another crime (e.g., hacking, cracking, and/or computer sabotage, etc.). Second, the computer is the tool used or is integral to the commission of the crime. This includes online fraud, theft or embezzlement. Cyberstalking, forgery and the dissemination of child pornography would also fall under this category of cybercrime. Third, the computer is only an incidental aspect of the crime. In other words, the computer itself was not necessary for commission of the crime, but connected in some way. For example, a computer may be a source of evidence in cases where an offender stores his or her criminal transactions on the computer. This article focuses on the first two categories and adopts the following definition of cybercrime. "Cybercrime can be regarded as computer-mediated activities which are either illegal or considered illicit by certain parties and which can be conducted through global electronic networks."

The Origins of Cybercrime

Although several types of cybercrime are similar in nature to traditional crimes (e.g., online theft is still theft), cybercrime is a relatively new phenomenon. In fact, cybercrime itself would not be possible without the proliferation of and human reliance upon computers. Computers control nearly every aspect of our lives: the operation of cars, the flow of data in business, and most importantly, the services vital to economic growth and national security. These services or "critical infrastructures" include telecommunications, banking and finance, transportation (i.e., roads, railroads and airports), electrical energy, gas and oil supply, water supply, emergency services (i.e., fire, health and police), and government operations. Where in the past these services depended very little on computers, they now completely rely on them for control, management and interaction amongst themselves. In addition, cybercrime would be impossible without the Internet. Conceptualized in 1966, the ARPA [Advanced Research Projects Agency] office of the Department of Defense began construction of the Internet in 1969. A few years later, the first e-mail system was developed and multiple networks began connecting with one another. Throughout the 1980's only scientists and academicians used the Internet. In 1990, the World Wide Web (WWW) was created and the Department of Defense transferred control over to the National Science Foundation and private carriers. Since then, primarily private and commercial parties utilize the Internet. Internationally, there are more than 430 million Internet users. Regionally, this includes 1.8 million African users (1,400 persons online per 100,000), 96 million Asian users (3,600 online per 100,000), 140 million European users (20,000 online per 100,000), 7.3 million

Middle Eastern users (3,340 online per 100,000), 166 million North American users (39,000 online per 100,000), 8.3 million Oceanic users (8,000 online per 100,000) and 11.8 million South American users (4,100 online per 100,000). The United States alone accounts for more than 90% of the North American online population and 38% of the international online population (54,000 online per 100,000). A study of over 500 American businesses conducted by the Computer Security Institute (CSI), found that 98% of the companies maintained WWW sites and over half of them conducted electronic commerce on the Internet. . . . Web statistics compiled [in 2002] by InterGOV, an international research organization with staff and management from around the world, indicates that companies use the Internet primarily for advertising, marketing, public relations, and customer service. Nevertheless, the rise in popularity of the Internet for both private persons and businesses has resulted in a corresponding rise in the number of Internet-related crimes.

The Cost and Scope of Cybercrime

International estimates indicate that cybercrime costs approximately $50 billion annually. More specifically, cybercrime costs the United States more than $5 billion per year. In England, cybercrime is estimated to cost approximately 250 million pounds or $417.7 million annually. Moreover, the worldwide market for information security products is expected to total $17 billion by the year 2003. Thus far in 2002, InterGOV has received 1.4 million criminal and civil complaints concerning cybercrime related activities. This amounts to nearly 3,704 complaints per day (an increase of 41% when compared to 2001). The 2002 United States Computer Crime and Security Survey found that 90% of the respondents (mostly companies) suffered from computer security breaches within the last 12 months. More than half indicated their Internet connection as a frequent point of attack. The researchers also reported that 80% of the respondents indicated substantial financial loss due to computer security breaches. The 2002 Australian Computer Crime and Security Survey found that approximately 67% of Australian businesses polled within the last 12 months [since 2001] suffered from a computer security incident and over 70% were forced to significantly increase information security expenditures, compared with the previous year. Although all of the above research organizations report highly unfavorable statistics, one must keep in mind that many break-ins, if actually detected, go unreported. In fact, only about 10% of all cyber-crimes committed are actually reported and fewer than 2% re-sult in a conviction. This is primarily due to two reasons. First, businesses and financial institutions feel that they have more to lose by reporting computer security breaches. They argue that customers will lose confidence in the company if business and financial transactions are known to be insecure. Second, a majority of cybercrime victims do not report crimes against them, assuming that law enforcement will provide little or no assistance. Unfortunately, these victims may be correct in their assumptions.

The Failure of Law Enforcement

Kenneth Rosenblatt, Deputy District Attorney for Santa Clara, California, states: "I think it is going to take a lot of people dy-ing, unfortunately, before anything will be done about com-puter crime." Globally, cybercrime is not a priority for most po-lice departments. Reasons for this international lack of concern include scarce resources, insufficient training and fear of tech-nology, lack of public outcry, and the police culture itself. For example, training officers to investigate cybercrime requires an extensive and ongoing educational program. In addition, the equipment necessary to investigate cybercrime is expensive and must be updated constantly. Third, public crime polls in-dicate that people are more concerned with and would rather have police investigate rapes, murders, thefts and drugs. Fi-nally, because heroism, physical bravery, and catching violent offenders are rewarded, police departments intentionally or unintentionally place a lower value on apprehending non-violent offenders. Other issues impeding law enforcement in-clude serious jurisdictional problems, difficulty in obtaining digital evidence, and possible infringement on privacy rights. The remainder of this article discusses specific types of cyber-crime. In doing so, both crimes in which the computer is the target of criminal activity and offenses in which the computer is the tool used in the commission of the crime, are addressed.

Cybercrimes That Target Computers

Computer network break-ins: Crimes in which the computer or computer system is the target of criminal activity include com-

puter network break-ins, industrial espionage, computer sabotage, and cyberterrorism (as discussed previously). The term
"computer network break-in" is a general term encompassing
several different activities. These activities include first breaking
into a computer system (i.e., from a remote location) and then
proceeding to steal data, plant viruses, change usernames and
passwords, manipulate web pages, or just simply explore the
network. In the United States, network intrusions are illegal at
the federal level. Nonetheless, detection is extremely difficult.

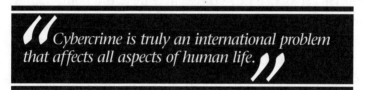

Cybercrime is truly an international problem that affects all aspects of human life.

Industrial espionage: Undoubtedly, corporations compete to
be first at developing new and desired products and then successfully selling those products. Therefore, it is imperative that
competitors know what the competition is doing. Where in the
past obtaining information (i.e., legally or illegally) concerning
competitor product development, finances, research, and marketing strategies was time-consuming and difficult, today's
globally networked society allows companies to electronically
spy on one another and gather information more quickly. In
fact, computer network break-ins that result in the unauthorized viewing or theft of corporate information are defined as
industrial espionage. Industrial espionage is difficult to detect
and rarely results in a conviction.

Computer sabotage: Most everybody who uses a computer
has been a victim of computer sabotage. The goal of computer
sabotage is to hinder the normal functioning of a computer or
computer system. This is accomplished primarily through the
creation and dissemination of computer viruses and worms. Although the terms are used almost interchangeably, viruses and
worms differ from one another. A computer virus is a program
designed to infect executable files, essentially causing them to
function abnormally (e.g., deletion or alteration of important
files). Executable files include application programs, operating
systems, macros, and the boot sector of a computer hard drive.
Once a user runs the infected program, new copies of the virus
are automatically created and quickly spread from one ma-
chine to another. Thus, the virus causes harm and is copied,

only after an executable file is run. A worm, on the other hand, is a malicious program that makes copies of itself, without any assistance from a user. The goal of a worm is to make so many copies of itself that it eventually clogs disk drives and/or the Internet. Those who wish to slow the legitimate traffic of the Internet desire this malicious program. Moreover, it costs an estimated $1 million annually to clean worms and viruses off computers in the United States. The above cybercrimes involve activities where computers or computer systems are targets of criminal activity. Next, crimes in which the computer is the tool used in the commission of the crime are discussed.

Cybercrimes That Use Computers

Cyberstalking: Crimes in which the computer plays an integral part include cyberstalking, cyberfraud, software piracy, identity theft, and child pornography. According to the National Center for Victims of Crime (NCVC), "cyberstalking can be defined as threatening behavior or unwanted advances directed at another using the Internet and other forms of online communications." Estimates [made in 2002] indicate that there are more than 475,000 victims of cyberstalking each year. Cyberstalking activities include sending threatening or obscene e-mail, chatroom harassment and/or verbal abuse, and sending improper messages and requests via e-mail. Cyberstalkers usually target women and children (e.g., over 90% of the victims are women), and many victims experience psychological trauma and eventual physical harm.

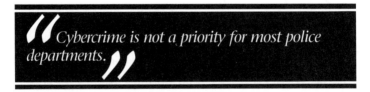

Cybercrime is not a priority for most police departments.

Cyberfraud: According to the FBI's Internet Fraud and Complaint Center, "Internet fraud is defined as any fraudulent scheme in which one or more components of the Internet, such as Web sites, chat rooms and e-mail, play a significant role in offering nonexistent goods or services to consumers, communicating false or fraudulent representations about the schemes to consumers, or transmitting victims' funds, access devices or other items of value to the control of the scheme's perpetrators." Internet fraud encompasses all of the following: Internet auction fraud (64% of all Internet fraud reported), Internet service provider fraud, fraudulent Internet website design services, multi-level marketing fraud, business opportunities and work-at-home schemes, get-rich-quick schemes, travel fraud, and health-care fraud. Internationally, Internet fraud costs an average $110,000 per corporate/organization victim and at least $15,000 on average per individual victim.

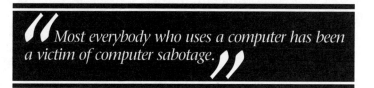

Most everybody who uses a computer has been a victim of computer sabotage.

Software piracy: According to Microsoft, software piracy is defined "as the copying of a computer software program without the permission of the copyright owner." This may include making unlicensed copies of software and/or under-reporting the number of installed copies in volume-licensing agreements. Recent estimates indicate that more than $7.5 billion worth of American software is illegally copied and distributed around the world each year. In China, 96% of all business software is pirated. Vietnam surpasses that, with over 98% of all business software reported as pirated.

Identity theft: "Every 79 seconds, a thief steals someone's identity, opens accounts in the victim's name and goes on a buying spree." According to the Identity Theft Resource Center, "identity theft is a crime in which an imposter obtains key pieces of information such as Social Security and driver's license numbers to obtain credit, merchandise and services in the name of the victim. The victim is left with a ruined credit history and the time-consuming and complicated task of regaining financial health. The imposter may even use the victim's good name for criminal activities." Last year [2001], an estimated 700,000 Americans were victims of identity theft. Internationally, stolen and posted credit card numbers cost credit card companies an estimated $3 billion in 2001.

Child pornography: To conclude, this article addresses a type of cybercrime that is probably the source of most public concern. Recent estimates indicate that the child pornography industry makes $2–3 billion annually (7% of the pornography industry in the U.S.). "Child pornography has been defined under federal statute as a visual depiction of a minor engaged in sexually explicit conduct." In America, most states prohibit creating, storing, and/or distributing child pornography (real or virtual) on computers. In addition, many states outlaw sending obscene material to children. Nonetheless, a recent study of a national representative sample of over 1,500 youths reported that 1 in 5 received a sexual solicitation over the Internet in the last 12 months. Likewise, 1 in 4 received unwanted pornographic images via e-mail. Unfortunately, the flexibility of the Internet and widespread use of encryption (i.e., scrambling data to prevent unauthorized viewing) makes it very difficult for law enforcement to apprehend these problematic individuals.

Clearly, cybercrime is a global problem that costs an estimated $50 billion annually. With the number of Internet users expected to reach 900 million by 2004, the number of victims and cost of cybercrime is sure to rise. Unfortunately, despite a few celebrated arrests, law enforcement officials around the world are either unable and/or unwilling to stop cybercrime.

Law Enforcement Is Developing New Ways to Fight Internet Crime

Peter Piazza

Peter Piazza is assistant editor of the American Society for Industrial Security's magazine Security Management.

Growing numbers of law enforcement task forces focusing on computer crime have developed in the United States in recent years. These task forces began with a few local efforts in the 1990s, but as Internet use and abuse both grew, the number of task forces increased and the groups began to communicate and support each other. More recently, state and federal law enforcement agencies have also established special units to fight interstate and international computer crime. These groups help to extend the reach of local forces and make it easier for the smaller groups to network with each other. Law enforcement officials fighting cybercrime still face significant challenges, including obtaining funding, managing growing caseloads, attracting qualified personnel, and, above all, creating trust between law enforcement and the private or business sector. Nonetheless, computer crime task forces have transformed the way law enforcement tackles cybercrime.

It was 10:30 in the morning when a message popped up on the computer screen of a 13-year-old girl in Northern California. The instant message was unsolicited, meaning the alleged sender—Christopher Andreas Georghiou, a 21-year-old man in

Turlock, California—was searching the profiles of young girls in his area. After a half hour of online chatting, the girl agreed to meet Georghiou.

Less than an hour after the first message was sent, Georghiou was in handcuffs and on his way to the Stanislaus County Jail for soliciting sex with a minor. But the "minor," in this case, was actually Stanislaus County Sheriffs Department Detective Ken Hedrick, a member of the Sacramento Valley Hi-Tech Crimes Task Force.

The Georghiou case is just one of many success stories to come out of the computer crime task forces that have blossomed across the United States in recent years. A variety of these collaborative efforts now exist, some cobbled together locally out of sheer necessity, others built carefully at the federal level to overcome the difficulties inherent in cybercrime investigations. All of these groups have members with a passion for technology and a devotion to fighting today's cyber criminals.

As these task forces have evolved over the past few years, significant progress has been made. But serious challenges lie ahead.

First Efforts to Fight Cybercrime

In the 1990s, even as the Internet was beginning its expansion from a network of bulletin boards to a globally connected information superhighway, computer crime was catching the attention of some local prosecutors and police officers separately but simultaneously across the country. The growth of these grassroots efforts was not unlike the expansion of the Internet itself: a core of computer aficionados building local ad hoc networks, then linking to other networks and gradually expanding their reach.

Bradley Gross, a former Miami-Dade County assistant state attorney and now an attorney with Becker & Polikoff, is one of these pioneers. He first became involved in prosecuting computer crimes in the early 1990s in Nassau County, New York, where he worked in the county district attorney's office.

"Because I had been, for lack of a better way of putting it, a computer nerd for 20 years or so, I was given the task of advising them on all computer cases that came in," he says. Gross prosecuted the nation's first cyberstalking case in 1994. Other cases included computer fraud and trespass issues.

Gross moved to Florida and went to work for the economic

crime division of the state attorney's office. Along with a team of detectives originally trained in investigating cellular-phone fraud, Gross set up a task force known as the Special Investigation Unit for Internet and Computer Fraud in 1999. It was tough going at first, he says, because resources and time were scarce.

"It was a one-man show," he remembers. "I had the support of the office in that they gave me the time and leeway to pursue these kinds of cases, but there was no money allotted just to investigating these types of crime." The detectives who worked with him had to split their time between his unit and units that worked on more traditional crimes.

A vast gray area of [cybercrime] cases . . . were floating around.

Gross and his team soon discovered that there was no shortage of crimes to prosecute. His unit became involved with "a vast gray area of cases that were floating around, people getting ripped off in more than a de minimus [inconsequential] fashion that no one was doing anything about."

The gray area existed for several reasons, including a lack of understanding about the nature of these crimes and a lack of resources available to law enforcement agencies, according to Gross. Most police agencies back then tended to shrug online fraud off as a civil matter, he says, or they left it to federal agencies.

But the federal agencies adhered to an unwritten rule that they would only pursue cases where the amount of the loss or the type of defendant met a certain threshold, because resources were limited. As a result, people who had been victimized for what they considered a large amount of money (tens of thousands of dollars) were left without a place to go for help, says Gross.

Once Gross's unit began to investigate these crimes, it was quickly apparent that they needed more resources than were available; because cases were crossing jurisdictional boundaries, the unit needed the assistance of other law enforcement agencies. "We simply didn't have the manpower or resources to go and cross over several jurisdictional lines to conduct an investigation 100 or 200 miles away from where we were, but where the effects [of the crime] were being felt," Gross says.

Members of the unit went to meet with their colleagues in other Florida police departments to try to develop cost-effective means of dealing with multijurisdictional cases. Before long, police officers with similar interests in computers and cybercrime throughout the state were contacting each other for help, building networking opportunities out of necessity.

Task Forces Help Each Other

But interest in what the team was doing quickly moved beyond Florida. Investigators from other states who heard about the unit's efforts and who wanted to set up similar investigative and prosecutorial units were soon visiting, Gross says, to discuss how the unit worked. Once these other jurisdictions established their own units, they became a resource for each other, and lines of communication—phone, fax, e-mail, and in particular listservs (online mailing lists of subscribers)—were established, connecting the unit's members with other local and state task forces, as well as agents from the FBI and the Secret Service.

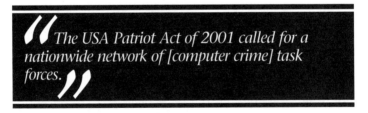

The USA Patriot Act of 2001 called for a nationwide network of [computer crime] task forces.

Great minds think alike. Gross's efforts were duplicated a state away. Steve Edwards, the special agent in charge of the Georgia Bureau of Investigation's (GBI's) Financial Investigations Unit, explains that the Georgia State Computer Crimes Task Force was born as the financial services sector began to switch to computers [around 1990]. Edwards says, "We'd been doing financial investigations for years, and often we'd go to a crime scene and we were looking for the paper evidence and there wouldn't be any," but there would be a computer. "Through evolution," he says, "we came to the realization that we needed to seize these computers, do computer forensics, and get the evidence properly."

Once the Georgia unit began to gain expertise in computer seizures and forensics, they started getting requests for help, and soon the team was assisting in homicide and drug cases where computers might hold evidence. Soon, Edwards says, the state was offering some additional resources and asking the unit to expand. But the task force still operates on a shoestring. . . .

Federal Agencies Lend a Hand

Many law enforcement agencies at the federal level have also established computer crime units to target multistate or even international crimes, such as those committed by identity-theft rings. But these agency-specific units sometimes overlap with the jurisdictions of similar units within other federal agencies. For example, the FBI has a special investigative unit for computer crimes targeting children, as does the U.S. Customs Service. These units also sometimes need to coordinate with state and local organizations, such as those already discussed. Some programs have been established to better coordinate all of these resources.

One such program is the Secret Service's Electronic Crimes Task Force (ECTF) initiative, which is one of the largest and most well known efforts to provide a "one-stop shop" for federal and local law enforcement agencies tasked with fighting computer crimes.

In the ECTF model, specially trained Secret Service agents bring together diverse members to find and share resources and knowledge.

Knowing who to go to for help when a cybercrime occurs is critical.

For example, the first ECTF, established in New York City in 1995, comprises a community of 50 federal, state, and local law enforcement agencies and more than 200 corporations, as well as prosecutors and academic leaders. The NYECTF has made more than 860 arrests involving electronic crime losses in excess of $730 million. It has also trained more than 13,000 law enforcement personnel, prosecutors, and private-industry personnel.

High-profile cases it has been involved with include the prosecution of John Gotti, Jr., in 1999 and the 2001 case of multiple identity thefts by a New York City busboy who stole personal financial information of celebrities chosen from the Forbes list of the 400 richest people in America. He used that information to try to transfer money from their online brokerage accounts to fraudulent accounts.

The NYECTF has been so successful that the USA Patriot Act of 2001 called for a nationwide network of task forces based on the New York model; eight more now exist across the country, from Boston to San Francisco.

Progress is being made elsewhere as well. After the Patriot Act was passed, the Secret Service expanded its efforts to help state and local agencies increase their skills in computer forensics investigations, says John Large, assistant special agent in charge of the Secret Service's Miami field office.

The biggest challenge is developing trust between public and private groups.

One "train the trainer" program that the Miami ECTF carried out proved particularly popular, Large says. "We took five or six local detectives from various cities and paid for their training" so that they received forensic skills identical to Secret Service agents. Trainees "also received $100,000 worth of equipment after completing the training" with which they could conduct forensic exams, Large says.

Extending Law Enforcement's Reach

John Frazzini, now vice president of intelligence operations with iDefense, a private intelligence security firm in Virginia, was until recently a Secret Service agent working with the ECTF. Frazzini founded the Washington, D.C., electronic crime task force and helped develop other Secret Service task forces nationwide. He says that federal initiatives differ from local ones in many ways, but the most important is scope.

"Oftentimes the state-run task forces focus on smaller-level crimes, such as smaller identity theft crimes, whereas the federal task forces are focused much more on transnational major crimes," he says. "State task forces don't necessarily have the reach to be able to conduct investigations beyond their jurisdiction; that's where they could leverage their association with the Secret Service task forces, in order to have a broader reach."

For example, he says, if a local police officer investigating an identity theft case needs to collect information on a hacker located in Eastern Europe, obtaining that information will be difficult or impossible; however, if the officer is working through a federal task force, more resources are available and it becomes more likely that the information can be obtained. . . .

Sharing Information

Some federal efforts, such as the FBI's InfraGard program, offer what cybercrime experts say is the most important advantage of computer crime task forces: networking opportunities. As Frazzini explains, knowing who to go to for help when a cybercrime occurs is critical, whether you're in law enforcement or in a private company.

An ancillary benefit of the task-force model is that it facilitates information sharing among law enforcement officials and prosecutors at the local level, says W.R. McKenzie, deputy district attorney from the Stanislaus [California] County District Attorney's office. Detectives learn the latest trends both with regard to what criminals are doing and with regard to the investigative techniques that law enforcement agencies are using, he says.

This model has also changed the way in which investigators and prosecutors work together, says McKenzie. When a crime such as a homicide or robbery takes place, detectives investigate and then report to the DA's office. But with crimes investigated through the task force, "as a prosecutor I can get involved in the cases at a much earlier stage. We can talk about what's the best way to investigate," he says. Ultimately if the cases end up at trial, "we want to make sure we've got the best investigation up front that we could have," says McKenzie. When they achieve that goal, he says, the cases often get settled out of court.

Facing Challenges

While these various task forces have begun to accomplish their missions with increasing skill and efficiency, significant challenges remain. Major concerns include acquiring funding, managing increasing caseloads, and finding qualified personnel. Another major challenge is building trust between the public and private sectors. . . .

Developing Trust

Without question, the biggest challenge is developing trust between public and private groups. "If the trust level is not elevated between the private sector and law enforcement, those task force environments will not work, period," asserts Frazzini. Companies have to trust that "when they come to law enforcement with their darkest secrets, that law enforcement is going to handle it in an appropriate way that's not going to re-victimize them."

This has long been a point of contention between businesses that suffer a cybercrime attack and law enforcement agencies whose officials fret that without information from victims, cybercriminals will never be brought to justice. Michael Overly, CISSP [member of Certified Information Systems Security Professionals], a partner in the e-Business and Information Technology Practice at the law firm of Foley & Gardner, says that law enforcement has made some positive changes, in part thanks to the increasing popularity of programs such as ECTF and InfraGard.

"There was a clear perception in private industry that many of the computer crimes units were essentially a bull in a china shop when they would do these investigations," Overly explains. Now, he says, "I think they have absolutely realized that and they are working very hard to overcome that reputation."

Despite their advancements, investigators are still only scratching the surface of cybercrime. Alan Paller, director of research for the SANS Institute [a major provider of information security training], notes that the increased effort to have successful prosecutions and tougher sentences, plus laws that make tracking Web-based criminals easier, is a giant step in the right direction.

In less than a decade, computer crime task forces have transformed the way in which law enforcement investigates a host of crimes. But when asked if law enforcement is winning the war on cybercrime, Sergeant [Adam] Christianson [who supervises a satellite office of the Sacramento Valley, California, High-Tech Task Force, which specializes in computer crimes] admits, "We're just barely keeping our heads above the water."

3

Hacking for Dollars

Adam Piore et al.

Adam Piore, the general editor of Newsweek *and an expert on international affairs, headed the team of reporters who contributed to this article.*

Cybercrime is becoming the province of sophisticated, ruthless criminals in many countries. The lone hacker, interested mainly in exploring computer systems and rebelling against authority, is being replaced by organized gangs that primarily want to make money. Examples of this new breed include a young Russian hacker who stole $300,000 from American corporations in a single year. Computer criminals like this hacker use a variety of tricks, ranging from viruses to fake Web sites that imitate those of trusted companies. They are hard to catch, not only because of their skill but because many countries do not have or do not enforce antihacking laws. Computer users, especially individuals and small businesses, must be extremely vigilant if they want to protect themselves from these clever criminals.

In the high-tech battlefield of cyberspace, the thirtysomething Russian with the jet black goatee and the new denim coat considers himself a freedom fighter—a descendant of those legendary computer geeks whose cyberstunts drove the establishment wild and helped define a unique Internet culture. Like his hacker predecessors, he has his own subversive code, this one tinged with the slogans of anti-globalization. He talks of "freedom," "the unhindered flow of ideas" and the need to break the stranglehold of "monster corporations like Microsoft." (He won't hack into Russian companies.) "I live in the shadows. That is

Adam Piore, Frank Brown, Nadezhda Titova, Mike Kepp, Sarah Sennott, B.J. Lee, Barbie Nadeau, and Craig Simons, "Hacking for Dollars," *Newsweek International*, December 22, 2003, p. 48. Copyright © 2003 by Newsweek, Inc. Reproduced by permission.

where I want to be," says the hacker—we'll call him Dmitry—over a late-night meal in a Moscow restaurant. "I don't need to prove anything to anyone."

Dig a little deeper and you'll find there's something that differentiates this New Age cybersurfer from his high-minded brethren. Last year Dmitry netted $300,000—stolen from major American corporations. Like a slick businessman, Dmitry arrives for his secret rendezvous with *NEWSWEEK* accompanied by his lawyer. He works as part of a hacker team, composed of 10 or so experienced criminals, each with his own specialty. His job: to break into networks, opening the way for his confederates to steal and decode company information. He'll work 16-hour days for six months preparing for an assault on a Western corporation that might last just minutes. "It's like a military attack," he says. "At first you do intelligence. You watch their behavior. You get ready for X-Hour. When you're 90 percent sure of success, you attack."

The days when the lone hacker was the symbol of all that was good about the Internet seem to be fading fast. Dmitry is part of perhaps the fastest growing criminal enterprise of the 21st century. These hardened pros are well schooled in the arts of extortion, fraud and intellectual-property theft. Sure, many retain some of the rebellious affectations of their predecessors by wrapping themselves in anti-establishment, anti-globo speak. But they're increasingly organized, sophisticated and often ruthless. And they are costing companies and individuals billions of dollars. A growing number of them live far beyond the clutches of U.S., Japanese or European law-enforcement officials, in places like Russia, Brazil, China and South Korea. From distant domains they route their signals through multiple countries to throw the digital cops off their trail, then they hack into the files of large corporations or individuals and steal. "This is increasing at an alarming rate," says Harold M. Hendershot, an official in the FBI's cyberdivision. "It used to be that hackers claimed to want to point out societal vulnerabilities—they actually claimed to be doing it for the benefit of society. But now more and more criminals are realizing that information is power, power is money, and knowledge is easy to get if you break into the right systems."

The problem has been germinating for years. Identity fraud, in which hackers glean information from the Internet to get free credit cards and make deals under another's name—displaced run-of-the-mill scams as the U.S. Federal Trade Commission's top problem in 2001. Last year the FTC got 219,000 complaints, and expects a tenfold rise by 2005. Even more alarming is the spike in wire fraud, credit-card theft, stolen trade secrets and extortion.

How much money is being stolen? Estimates are hard because many victims—especially banks and other corporations—are reluctant to speak about their losses. By most accounts though, the problem is growing rapidly. Mi2g, a computer-security firm, puts the worldwide economic damage from digital attacks at between $37 billion and $45 billion in 2002. Other estimates fix the damage for 2003 at $135 billion. It's no longer just Westerners being hit. According to one survey, 77 percent of executives at Brazil's largest companies reported problems with cybercrime security in the past six months, up 43 percent from the previous year. In Russia, computer-related crime cost Internet users an estimated $6 billion in 2002—triple the year before.

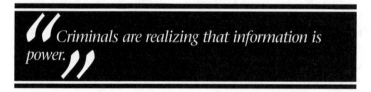

Criminals are realizing that information is power.

It seems odd that Internet crime would have risen steeply since the September 11 attacks, when security became a priority for most organizations. Criminal gangs, it seems, have only just begun to realize how much money can be made. They're either learning how to hack the Internet themselves or are recruiting ambitious young hackers to do their dirty work for them. The Internet is reaching more of the world's have-nots, tempting them to turn it against rich Western corporations. In January, 59 million Chinese used the Internet regularly, a 2,800 percent rise from 1998, according to the China Internet Network Information Center. Although that's a fraction of China's 1.3 billion people, the country has already become one of the fastest growing hacker havens. Russian hackers for hire complain that their Chinese counterparts are driving down prices for their services, by charging 10 to 50 percent less.

The result is a growing onslaught on legitimate Internet users. The average U.S. company is now attacked 30 times a week, according to security firm Symantec Corp. Most are efforts to scan for vulnerabilities, but about 15 percent are actual attacks. The number of Web-site violations reported to Carnegie

Mellon's Internet-security center jumped to 114,855 this year from 82,094 last year. The number of software holes reported in the nation's computer networks grew by 80 percent in 2002, says Symantec. "There is a cat-and-mouse game going on," says George Bakos, security expert at Dartmouth's Institute for Security Technology Studies. "Unfortunately we would fall into the category of mice: we're the target. The hackers keep coming up with new ways to go after us."

Alexey Ivanov is typical of these new hackers. He began fooling around on computers at the age of 7 and scored at the genius level on intelligence tests. But there isn't much opportunity in Chelyabinsk, Russia, a depressed area in the Ural Mountains, even for a computer whiz. Ivanov dropped out of college because he couldn't afford the tuition and got a job as a furniture mover. He "recognized the obvious, that [his furniture-moving job] was a dead end and a complete waste of his professional-level skills with computers," says his attorney, Morgan Rueckert. So in the spring of 2000, Ivanov joined a team of other computer experts and set to work hacking corporate Web sites. New servers have passwords that are set by default at the factory, and some corporations don't bother to change them. Ivanov knew the passwords for Microsoft NT servers, and would scan the Net for vulnerable servers. When he found one, he'd hack in to steal credit-card numbers.

Ivanov and his cohorts quickly moved on to more sophisticated scams. Using a practice called "spoofing," he created a Web site he called "Pay Pai" that looked exactly like Pay Pal's site. Then he and his gang would send e-mails to Pay Pal users telling them to contact the site to collect credit, and offering a link to the Pay Pai site—where they'd enter their credit card numbers. Such attacks, known as "phishing," are common nowadays—18 banks in Australia, New Zealand, the United States and Great Britain have been hit in the past six months.

Computer viruses have become a standard tool of hacker criminals. Hackers send them out to infect vulnerable computers, turning them into "zombies" that can then be manipulated to launch attacks, or using Trojan horse viruses that surreptitiously cull credit-card data, passwords or other sensitive information. Just like the mythical equine of old, a hacker horse usually comes as an e-mail attachment masquerading as something tempting, such as "sex.movie.mpg." Opening the attachment activates a program that gives the hacker access to the contents of the infected computer and the ability to control it.

Last month in Brazil, police arrested 28 hackers in four states who had stolen more than $10 million using a Trojan horse disguised as a "You've Just Won a Trip" promotion.

Hackers have lately begun to exploit fear to extort money from would-be victims. Ivanov and his team used this technique to blackmail Web-site owners from Seattle to Connecticut, threatening to expose their security vulnerabilities if they did not wire cash to Russia. In a spate of recent cases, criminal gangs overseas have begun threatening to launch distributed-denial-of-service attacks (DDS), flooding a server with so much incoming data that it crashes. In September, more than a dozen offshore betting sites serving the U.S. market were reportedly brought down by DDS attacks. The attackers then followed with e-mails—demanding payments of up to $40,000—though extortion schemes can run as high as $500,000. The *Financial Times* reported that investigators, who traced the assaults back to St. Petersburg, believe the Russian mafia was running the show.

There's increasing evidence that organized crime is moving in on Internet crime.

Indeed, there's increasing evidence that organized crime is moving in on Internet crime. Ivanov and his confederate Sergey Gorshkov were known to be attached to a sophisticated criminal ring. They reportedly paid 30 percent to a guardian, who oversaw a loosely knit network of hacker criminal cells. In Italy, considered a major hacker hub, "there are strong rumors that the Italian mafia is directly involved," says Dario Forte of Italy's elite Guardia di Finanza. Brazil has also long been a breeding ground for organized-criminal gangs, who take advantage of lax laws. According to mi2g, 18 of the world's 20 most active hacking groups are based in Brazil.

The foot soldiers of these new cybercrime gangs appear to be either young, precocious kids or frustrated men in their 20s or 30s. They're increasingly likely to hail from developing countries with rampant unemployment, and to see their computer skills as a ticket to opportunity. Most of them are probably recruited by criminal groups through Internet chat rooms. One South Korean crime group held a bogus hacker contest and recruited from among the more promising contestants. By the time Korean police busted them last month, their ranks had swelled to 4,400 hackers, who had broken into the Internet servers of more than 90 government offices and private firms and stolen the personal information of more than 2.6 million people. All told, hacker crimes have soared in Korea from 449 in 2000 to 14,065 last year, according to the National Police Agency.

So why can't law enforcement stop cybercrimes? For one thing, hackers are elusive. Just as mafiosi will launder money to disguise its source, sophisticated cybercriminals disguise their origin. "If I'm going to hack your system in New York, I would probably hack into four or five systems worldwide first to disguise myself," says the FBI's Hendershot. "I would pick countries where I know the laws aren't as great to investigate crimes, or maybe [the United States doesn't] have the best international relations."

The FBI grew so frustrated with the lack of cooperation from Russia's cybercops, it resorted to desperate measures to nab Ivanov. Through a phony computer-security company in Seattle, FBI investigators asked him to fly there for a job interview. Ivanov jumped at the chance to escape Russia, even offering to bring his cohort Gorshkov. When the pair arrived, they put on a computer-security demonstration for the undercover cops, using tools from their own Web sites back home. This time, it was the FBI who captured Ivanov's and Gorshkov's keystrokes, broke into their computers and downloaded evidence. The hackers had been hacked.

The FBI may have nabbed Ivanov and Gorshkov—Ivanov is serving his jail sentence near Hartford, Connecticut, having pleaded guilty to hacking into 16 Web sites—and attempting to extort money; Gorshkov got off with a 15-month sentence—but the conviction came at a price. The Russians were furious at the stunt. They accused the FBI of illegally obtaining evidence and indicted the agents working the case of crimes in Russia. The FBI recently offered $100,000 for hardware, software and training to Russian agents, but they are unlikely to make much headway against the hackers. Hacking into U.S. systems isn't illegal in Russia. Ivanov's crime ring is still believed to be intact.

The lack of antihacking laws is not unique to Russia. China's laws regarding cybercrime are inadequate, say officials. Brazil's legislation provides for paltry incarceration rates and enforcement is lax. The EU has drafted laws similar to those in the United States, but has yet to ratify them. In Hendershot's opinion, only the United States and Britain have laws that come even close to adequate in defining cybercrimes and leveling penalties.

What can companies and home-computer users do to protect themselves? Vigilance is the only option. Corporations—particularly small- and medium-size ones—could do better at availing themselves of new software that plugs security holes in antiquated servers, such as new products introduced last year to deter certain kinds of spoofing scams. And whereas large corporations generally hire security experts to scan their software and computers to make sure that any backdoor administrative passwords are deleted, most small- and mid-size companies don't bother. Individual computer users can be even more vulnerable. "There are so many industry-best practices not being implemented by home users," says Dartmouth's Bakos. Among the recommended practices are using firewalls and security software. Says Lee Byong Ki, police chief in charge of cybercrimes in South Korea: People "need to understand that as soon as their server is connected to the Internet, their information is exposed to hacker attacks."

In retrospect, it seems naive to expect a network of networks, designed not for security but to be open to all, to remain free of the criminal element for very long. Almost from the beginning, the Internet has embraced the good and the bad, the inspiring and the mundane. Perhaps it's only natural that criminals are at last taking up a place, too. How long it will take for lawmakers and police to catch up with them is anybody's guess. But when they do, the Internet is apt to be a much different place than what it started out to be.

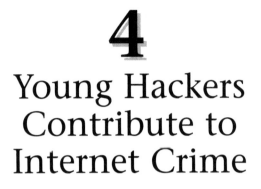

4

Young Hackers Contribute to Internet Crime

Arthur L. Bowker

Arthur L. Bowker writes frequently for the FBI Law Enforcement Bulletin, *in which the following article originally appeared.*

Since the late 1990s, the number and seriousness of computer crimes committed by young people have greatly increased. Several factors contribute to this growth, including teenagers' rapidly increasing technical knowledge and an accompanying apparent deficit in ethics. Juvenile delinquency involving computers results in substantial costs to society. Law enforcement officials encounter a number of problems in handling juvenile computer crime cases, including disputes about jurisdiction and the difficulty of determining which actions should be considered criminal. Prevention, especially through education, is the best way to control juvenile computer crime.

In Chesterfield County, Virginia, a 16-year-old pleaded guilty to computer trespassing for hacking into an Internet provider's system, causing $20,000 in damage. Five boys, ages 14 to 17, pleaded guilty to charges stemming from counterfeiting money on one of the youth's home computers. A 14-year-old boy in Mount Prospect, Illinois, pleaded guilty to possession of child pornography after downloading child pornographic images onto

Arthur L. Bowker, "The Advent of the Computer Delinquent," *FBI Law Enforcement Bulletin*, December 2000, pp. 7–11.

his computer. Five juveniles faced federal adjudication for hacking into computers at the Pentagon and NASA, accidentally shutting down an airport's runway lights, and stealing passwords from an Internet provider.

These and other incidents illustrate the types of computer delinquency that have become commonplace in a technologically advanced society. What has led to this problem, and what can the law enforcement community do to deter those of today's youth who have grasped the computer's usefulness in committing serious acts of delinquency?

Factors Contributing to Computer Delinquency

With the advent of the 21st century, new avenues of delinquency have begun to develop with each technological advance. Four factors contribute to these new avenues. First, today's youth possess more technological knowledge than any previous generation. They have grown up with the personal computer and the Internet. Due to this exposure, today's young people can conceive readily of the potential for both legitimate and illegitimate computer use.

Next, some evidence points to an apparent ethical deficit in today's youth, concerning appropriate computer use. For example, a 1997 study of undergraduate college students revealed that a substantial number had pirated software. Many of these students had gained illegal access to a computer system to either browse or exchange information. These findings proved similar to those of another study done 5 years earlier. The 1997 analysis further concluded that parents, and even teachers, may have advocated certain computer crimes, particularly software piracy. The study also noted that youths involved in computer crime, similar to other types of deviance, appeared to learn this behavior through interaction with their peers.

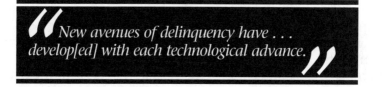

New avenues of delinquency have . . . develop[ed] with each technological advance.

Additionally, the peer groups that juveniles interact with have changed from school and neighborhood friends to a literal "global community." Unfortunately, this larger peer group contains hundreds of chat rooms, news groups, and Web sites advocating pedophilia, drugs, and hate and racist groups, along with information on identity falsification, credit card and check fraud, and computer hacking. Through these peer contacts, many juveniles learn about and support computer crimes.

A delinquent easily can use a computer to facilitate a five-figure . . . crime.

Finally, computers themselves make successful completion of certain acts of delinquency possible. Specifically, computer use over the Internet can conceal age and provide a degree of anonymity that did not exist previously. Youths not old enough to operate a motor vehicle can use their computers—in their own bedrooms, after curfew—to break into a system in another country. While in the past children may have had difficulty making fraudulent purchases, today they can go on-line and easily purchase those same age-restricted items by avoiding any suspicions based on their youthful appearance. The computer also greatly facilitates their escape after the fraud becomes known. The power of the computer makes counterfeiting or check fraud, offenses that once required expensive equipment and extensive expertise, literally "child's play."

As all of these factors have come together, the number of juveniles who have direct access to a computer and the Internet has risen sharply. According to the Office of Justice Programs, more than 28 million children currently go on-line, and industry experts predict that more than 45 million young people will use the Internet by 2002. Other projections indicate that by the year 2002, almost 80 percent of American teenagers will have access to on-line material. This analysis also reveals that many parents do not provide careful oversight of this computer use. For example, depending on the age group (either from 11 through 15 or 16 through 18 years of age), 38 percent of the parents of the younger group and 9 percent of the parents of the older group reported that they sit with their children while they are on-line.

Sixty-eight percent of parents of on-line children between the ages of 11 and 15 said that they know which Web sites their children visit, while 43 percent of the parents of the 16- to 18-

year-olds reported similar knowledge. In addition, 54 percent of the parents of the younger group revealed that they permit unlimited on-line access for their children, while 75 percent of the parents of the older children said that they allowed such computer usage.

Costs of Computer Delinquency

The losses or damages that a delinquent can inflict have changed dramatically due to society's increasing dependence on computers. Traditionally, the actions of a single delinquent would cause very few losses, injuries, or deaths. In the past, for example, it proved almost impossible for a juvenile delinquent to steal the amount of funds that a white collar criminal, such as an embezzler, could purloin. Today, however, a delinquent easily can use a computer to facilitate a five-figure or other high-tech crime. The potential for disaster when a juvenile hacker disrupts or manipulates safety functions, such as traffic signals, air traffic control, floodgates, or power grids, constitutes an even more troubling prospect.

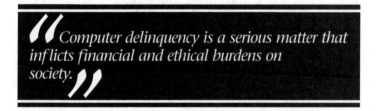

Computer delinquency is a serious matter that inflicts financial and ethical burdens on society.

Indirect costs of computer delinquency also require noting. "Innocent" juvenile exploration into computer systems can cause expensive systems to crash and inflict financial burdens to restore them. The prevalence of computer intrusions causes companies to take additional security measures and obtain special computer insurance, adding to the cost of goods and services. Computer delinquency also wastes investigative resources that agencies could better employ. For instance, an attack against defense computers could represent the work of juvenile "exploring" or an adult terrorist bent on destroying systems or stealing technology. Frequently, it takes a costly investigation to determine the suspects and their motives.

The jurisdictional concerns of technological crimes also makes adjudicating computer delinquents even more complicated than a typical delinquency case. Normally, adjudicating a delinquent takes place at the local level. Issues revolve around keeping the case in the juvenile court system or, if serious enough, a referral to the adult system. Typically, few juvenile cases involve multiple jurisdictions. However, a juvenile hacker can cross state boundaries and even international boundaries with the click of a mouse. Moreover, it is not inconceivable for future juvenile offenders to cause an international incident for hacking into an unfriendly foreign country's computer. The jurisdictional questions can begin to mount. Who handles these cases, the local authorities where the juvenile resides or the state or country of the target computer? Would federal prosecutors have an interest in the case? Who decides which jurisdiction will prosecute the case or whether the charge will be made in a juvenile or adult court?

Finally, some computer delinquents could become adult computer offenders. For example, several of the more infamous computer offenders began their criminal careers as juveniles. Also, [according to researcher J. Thomas McEwen,] research has shown that ". . . persons involved in computer crimes acquire their interest and skills at an early age. They are introduced to computers in school, and their usual 'career path' starts with illegally copying computer programs. Serious offenders then get into a progression of computer crimes including telecommunications fraud (making free long distance calls), unauthorized access to other computers (hacking for fun and profit), and credit card fraud (obtaining cash advances, purchasing equipment through computers)." Therefore, the entire criminal justice community must not ignore or downplay the significance of computer delinquency because these "wayward youths" may present future problems when they enter adulthood.

Law Enforcement Considerations

To effectively deal with the computer delinquent, law enforcement officers must make adequate preparations. They must not forget their skills and rules of evidence/procedure that they employ in investigating traditional delinquent behavior. Just because youngsters have mastered computer skills does not mean that they can comprehend their actions as against the law. For example, a 9-year-old who scans money for a school project does not warrant the same response as a 15-year-old who counterfeits and passes money. Investigators must establish that delinquents have some knowledge that their behavior is problematic. Do the delinquents conceal their computer actions from adults? Have they used passwords and encryption to protect their systems? Did they erase or destroy files to conceal their actions? What motivated them to commit the acts? Did they profit from their behavior? Was their offense committed to finance other delinquent behavior (e.g., drug use)? Have the youths exhibited similar behavior, either with or without a computer? What if officers uncover evidence on the youths' computers that indicate the delinquents have broken laws in several states or countries? Having answers to these questions will prepare law enforcement officers to present their findings to the appropriate parties for adjudication of the delinquents.

The issue of child pornography and the computer delinquent raises additional concerns for law enforcement officers. How should they respond to a 15-year-old male who has pornographic images of a 16-year-old female on his computer? What if this 15-year-old male is distributing these images to his friends? What about the 15-year-old male with pornographic images of an 8-year-old female on his computer? Where are they getting the images? Is an adult involved? Is the youth a victim of abuse? Law enforcement officers, in consultation with prosecutors, should consider such scenarios before they have to face them.

Teaching Computer Ethics

Law enforcement officers also should take a preventive approach to computer delinquency. Because of its potential to create havoc, computer delinquency warrants a serious preventive program aimed at the school-age child. In addition, the typical computer investigation is very time consuming and costly. Hence, the prevention of even one such investigation justifies the focus on educating youths regarding computer ethics. Researchers agree. "At one level, basic principles of computer ethics can be instilled in children (and adults) from the time of their initial introduction to information technology."

"A greater emphasis on computer ethics in school curricula might also contribute to heightened ethical awareness over time. Training in computing should be accompanied by an ethical component; information making it clear that intrusion and destruction is costly and harmful to individual human beings, and to society in general, not merely to amorphous organizations," [writes P.N. Grabosky and Russell G. Smith in *Crime in the Digital Age*].

Fortunately, basic tools exist for officers to use in developing a preventive program for children. Specifically, in 1991, the Computer Learning Foundation (CLF) and the U.S. Departments of Education and Justice began emphasizing the need to teach responsible computer use to children. The CLF began disseminating information to schools on methods for teaching children to become responsible computer users and developed the Code of Responsible Computing. In addition, the Department of Justice (DOJ) and the FBI have Web sites that contain information for children about appropriate computer use. DOJ's Web site also has a lesson plan for elementary and middle school teachers to use when covering computer crime and ethics with their students. Law enforcement officers could use these same materials to develop outreach programs for schools in their communities. Such programs also could include "cybersafety" tips to ensure that children do not fall victim to predators on the Internet.

The 21st century promises many technological changes for law enforcement. While some of these alterations will benefit the criminal justice community, such as the use of mapping technologies to determine crime trends, others, such as the emergence of computer delinquency, will produce negative challenges. Only by recognizing early on that computer delinquency is a serious matter that inflicts financial and ethical burdens on society can the criminal justice system hope to effectively handle these youths before they become master computer criminals.

5

Hackers Help to Prevent Internet Crime

Nick Wingfield

Nick Wingfield is a staff reporter at the Wall Street Journal's *San Francisco bureau.*

Many people think of computer hackers as criminals, but a new breed of "ethical hackers" earn their living by breaking into companies' computer systems at the companies' own request. Growing numbers of businesses are hiring these hackers to conduct vulnerability assessments, which reveal how the hackers' less ethical counterparts—or a company's own disgruntled employees—might access and damage computer networks. Company security officials are often shocked to learn how easy breaking into their systems can be. By finding security weaknesses, ethical hackers can reduce the risk of invasion; however, they can never completely eliminate it.

Usually, hackers and ethics don't mix.

These computer pros have become the scourge of just about any operation connected to the Internet. They break into computer networks and do all manner of trouble, most commonly defacing corporate or government Web sites with the digital equivalent of graffiti.

But there's another breed of hacker out there, one who works at foiling the efforts of the troublemakers. Unlike the hackers who attempt to break into corporate networks for sport and spying purposes, so-called ethical hackers typically hire themselves out to perform "vulnerability assessments" for clients—meaning they essentially break into the client's computer network with the client's consent in the interest of patching up security holes.

(A note on terminology: Although "ethical hacker" might seem a contradiction in terms to some, there is little agreement on the definition of the word "hacker." For many computer aficionados, "hacker" refers to an especially clever writer of software code and "cracker" refers to those who perform cyber-crimes.)

More companies are deciding it makes sense to pay the good guys to break into their networks before the bad guys do it and cause untold damage.

Ethical hackers are becoming a mainstay of the effort to make corporate networks more secure. Their appeal is simple: More companies are deciding it makes sense to pay the good guys to break into their networks before the bad guys do it and cause untold damage. The growth of the Internet has only added to the demand for vulnerability assessments, as companies have become more exposed to the outside world through the Web and finding security holes has become easier for mischief-makers because of readily available online hacker tools.

Companies ranging in size from start-ups to International Business Machines Corp. have ethical-hacking teams. Computer-security services, including vulnerability assessments by ethical hackers and other services, was a $1.8 billion world-wide market last year [2001] and is expected to grow at a compound annual rate of 28% [between 2002 and 2004] . . . according to Gartner Inc., a market-research firm in Stamford, Conn. Ethical hackers have become so mainstream they've even been immortalized on the silver screen—in the 1992 movie "Sneakers," starring Robert Redford as the head of a group of techno-wizards who test corporate security systems.

Closing the Gates

One of the biggest providers of ethical-hacking services is Computer Sciences Corp., or CSC, a technology consulting firm based in El Segundo, California.

If Hollywood were in charge of hiring the hackers at CSC, the staff would probably have nose rings—or at least wardrobes from somewhere with a bit more edge than Old Navy. There may be some element of truth to the stereotype of the ultrahip computer pro, fostered by movies like "Swordfish," but the image certainly doesn't apply to the 20 or so people who make up CSC's ethical-hacker team. The team's dress swings between business casual and suits—which may be due to the fact that the company's clients are usually big companies and government agencies like the Department of Defense.

"I'd love to be able to tell you we all look really wacky, but if that was the case we wouldn't be invited anywhere," says Jason Arnold, a senior computer scientist at CSC.

CSC's hackers don't completely lack color when they arrive for duty, though. "Sometimes we show up with dark glasses, just for fun," jokes David Klug, a network-security engineer at the company.

Jim Chapple, computer scientist principal at CSC, has the distinction of being both the leader of the hacker team and its oldest member, at age 45. Mr. Chapple doesn't oversee a bunch of truants, though: The rest of the team has a median age of about 30. Most of the ethical hackers are college educated, some were in the military, and many have worked for government agencies. A smattering of hackers also have government security clearances, which makes things easier when CSC is doing vulnerability assessments for secretive government agencies.

Although Mr. Chapple says some competitors differ on this point, he emphasizes that CSC doesn't hire reformed hackers—cyber-outlaws who crossed the law in the past but who've had a conversion. "Some of those hackers have turned totally ethical, [but] there have been some cases where they haven't," Mr. Chapple says. "We don't want to take the risk."

The Enemy Within

CSC's ethical hackers—most of whom work out of Annapolis Junction, Maryland—perform five to 10 vulnerability assessments a month. The assessments, which run a client anywhere from a few thousand dollars to over $100,000, can take two days to several weeks.

Mr. Chapple says there are essentially two broad categories of computer-security threats: external and internal. External threats range from industrial spies—who break into a company network over telephone lines or Internet connections to steal trade secrets—to hackers, who mostly sneak in to commit sabotage. But the most damaging, according to Mr. Chapple, are internal threats—from, say, disgruntled employees who wipe out company databases or spies who infiltrate the company and steal sensitive information.

"Many companies have what we call a candy type of security—a hard, crunchy shell and a soft, chewy center," he says. "The mentality is, 'We trust our employees.' What happens is, security becomes lax on the inside."

Scanning for Weak Spots

When CSC engineers show up at a client's offices to do a vulnerability assessment, the client usually gives the engineers little more than a physical cable so they can get connected to the network. The engineers are typically carting along a laptop loaded with software that goes by the ominous acronym Heat, for hydra expert assessment technology.

Team members use the Heat program, developed in-house by Mr. Chapple and others, to conduct broad scans of a client's network to identify all the hardware and software attached to it, from computer workstations to network routers to Web-site servers. Heat then automatically runs through a battery of vulnerability tests that identify and record security holes on the network.

Most . . . ethical hackers are college educated, some were in the military, and many have worked for government agencies.

This is another area where reality differs from Hollywood: In the movies, hackers such as the muscle-bound character played by Hugh Jackman in "Swordfish" sit before elegant flat-panel screens, manually performing security exploits by typing feverishly into their computers. In fact, in recent years hackers, ethical and otherwise, have come to depend more on automated tools that spool unspectacularly through a checklist of vulnerabilities.

For instance, Heat scans for known holes in Microsoft Corporation's popular Web-server software. A bad hacker could exploit the holes to post any content they want to on a company's Web site. Heat also scans for security holes in operating-system software that can allow a bad guy to gain untrammeled access to files on a corporate network.

Bad hackers routinely scan for such exploitable electronic loopholes—known as "exploits" in hacker jargon—and post software on the Internet that lets anyone scan for and take advantage of the vulnerabilities. CSC's security team updates the Heat software as new loopholes are publicized on the Internet.

The results of vulnerability assessments are sometimes shocking. Mr. Chapple says that his team invariably finds a security hole on clients' networks that gives the hackers wide sway to cause trouble. "Every customer that we have gone in and done an internal assessment for, we have been able for the most part to completely take over their networks," says Mr. Chapple.

Because a vulnerability assessment invariably ends up discovering security holes, most CSC clients don't want to talk about their assessments—and none of the clients want to be named. The head of information security at a large industrial company, who agreed to speak if he and his company weren't identified, hired CSC to do a vulnerability assessment two years ago and says the "findings were somewhat alarming." The CSC hackers were able to gain administrative privileges on the client's network, which gave them the ability (not acted upon, of course) to wreak havoc across the network.

Though the head of security says the assessment was very useful, he adds that such a test still can't prevent human error. "There were dumb errors caught through the scanning process," he says. If company technicians "had followed a checklist process, vulnerabilities wouldn't be introduced."

Missed Steps

Indeed, companies often fail to take seemingly obvious security precautions on their networks. On one assignment, for instance, CSC used a keystroke-monitoring program, which records all of the characters a user taps on a PC keyboard, to glean the password of a system administrator as he logged onto his computer. The system administrator's computer software could easily have been configured to prevent snooping by other users, but the capability hadn't been activated. Mr. Chapple says he was able to gain administrative privileges on the network through the monitoring program.

John Pescatore, a security analyst at Gartner, says consensual break-ins by ethical hackers are among the most thorough methods for conducting vulnerability assessments. But the trouble is that bad guys can do their own vulnerability assessments more frequently.

"The problem is hackers have unlimited time—it's like a hobby for them," says Mr. Pescatore. "If you're paying CSC [to do assessments] for a year, the hackers are scanning every day."

6

Cyberterrorism Is a Major Threat

The George W. Bush Administration

George W. Bush is the forty-third president.

The United States, like most developed nations, is completely dependent on computers and information technology. This dependence makes the country vulnerable to a new kind of terrorism. Tools for attacking the networked computers that control everything from banking to electricity are becoming more sophisticated, and they can be used from anywhere in the world. The threat of terrorist attacks against U.S. infrastructure, economy, and national security by means of computers is severe enough to require concerted protective efforts by government, business, and private citizens. Preventing cyberterrorist attacks is far better than trying to deal with them after they have happened.

The terrorist attacks against the United States that took place on September 11, 2001, had a profound impact on our Nation. The federal government and society as a whole have been forced to reexamine conceptions of security on our home soil, with many understanding only for the first time the lengths to which self-designated enemies of our country are willing to go to inflict debilitating damage.

We must move forward with the understanding that there are enemies who seek to inflict damage on our way of life. They are ready to attack us on our own soil, and they have shown a willingness to use unconventional means to execute those at-

The White House, "Cyberspace Threats and Vulnerabilities," *National Strategy to Secure Cyberspace*, February 2003, pp. 5–11.

tacks. While the attacks of September 11 were physical attacks, we are facing increasing threats from hostile adversaries in the realm of cyberspace as well.

For the United States, the information technology revolution quietly changed the way business and government operate. Without a great deal of thought about security, the Nation shifted the control of essential processes in manufacturing, utilities, banking, and communications to networked computers. As a result, the cost of doing business dropped and productivity skyrocketed. The trend toward greater use of networked systems continues. By 2003, our economy and national security became fully dependent upon information technology and the information infrastructure. A network of networks directly supports the operation of all sectors of our economy—energy (electric power, oil and gas), transportation (rail, air, merchant marine), finance and banking, information and telecommunications, public health, emergency services, water, chemical, defense industrial base, food, agriculture, and postal and shipping. The reach of these computer networks exceeds the bounds of cyberspace. They also control physical objects such as electrical transformers, trains, pipeline pumps, chemical vats, and radars.

Threats in Cyberspace

A spectrum of malicious actors can and do conduct attacks against our critical information infrastructures. Of primary concern is the threat of organized cyber attacks capable of causing debilitating disruption to our Nation's critical infrastructures, economy, or national security. The required technical sophistication to carry out such an attack is high—and partially explains the lack of a debilitating attack to date. We should not, however, be too sanguine. There have been instances where attackers have exploited vulnerabilities that may be indicative of more destructive capabilities.

Uncertainties exist as to the intent and full technical capabilities of several observed attacks. Enhanced cyber threat analysis is needed to address long-term trends related to threats and vulnerabilities. What is known is that the attack tools and methodologies are becoming widely available, and the technical capability and sophistication of users bent on causing havoc or disruption is improving.

As an example, consider the "NIMDA" ("ADMIN" spelled

backwards) attack. Despite the fact that NIMDA did not create a catastrophic disruption to the critical infrastructure, it is a good example of the increased technical sophistication showing up in cyber attacks. It demonstrated that the arsenal of weapons available to organized attackers now contains the capability to learn and adapt to its local environment. NIMDA was an automated cyber attack, a blend of a computer worm and a computer virus. It propagated across the Nation with enormous speed and tried several different ways to infect computer systems it invaded until it gained access and destroyed files. It went from nonexistent to nationwide in an hour, lasted for days, and attacked 86,000 computers.

Speed is also increasing. Consider that two months before NIMDA, a cyber attack called Code Red infected 150,000 computer systems in 14 hours.

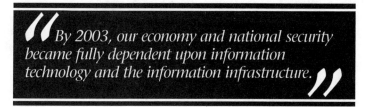

By 2003, our economy and national security became fully dependent upon information technology and the information infrastructure.

Because of the increasing sophistication of computer attack tools, an increasing number of actors are capable of launching nationally significant assaults against our infrastructures and cyberspace. In peacetime America's enemies may conduct espionage on our Government, university research centers, and private companies. They may also seek to prepare for cyber strikes during a confrontation by mapping U.S. information systems, identifying key targets, lacing our infrastructure with back doors and other means of access. In wartime or crisis, adversaries may seek to intimidate the Nation's political leaders by attacking critical infrastructures and key economic functions or eroding public confidence in information systems.

Cyber attacks on U.S. information networks can have serious consequences such as disrupting critical operations, causing loss of revenue and intellectual property, or loss of life. Countering such attacks requires the development of robust capabilities where they do not exist today if we are to reduce vulnerabilities and deter those with the capabilities and intent to harm our critical infrastructures.

Cyberspace provides a means for organized attack on our

infrastructure from a distance. These attacks require only commodity technology, and enable attackers to obfuscate their identities, locations, and paths of entry. Not only does cyberspace provide the ability to exploit weaknesses in our critical infrastructures, but it also provides a fulcrum for leveraging physical attacks by allowing the possibility of disrupting communications, hindering U.S. defensive or offensive response, or delaying emergency responders who would be essential following a physical attack.

In the last century, geographic isolation helped protect the United States from a direct physical invasion. In cyberspace national boundaries have little meaning. Information flows continuously and seamlessly across political, ethnic, and religious divides. Even the infrastructure that makes up cyberspace—software and hardware—is global in its design and development. Because of the global nature of cyberspace, the vulnerabilities that exist are open to the world and available to anyone, anywhere, with sufficient capability to exploit them.

While the Nation's critical infrastructures must, of course, deal with specific threats as they arise, waiting to learn of an imminent attack before addressing important critical infrastructure vulnerabilities is a risky and unacceptable strategy. Cyber attacks can burst onto the Nation's networks with little or no warning and spread so fast that many victims never have a chance to hear the alarms. Even with forewarning, they likely would not have had the time, knowledge, or tools needed to protect themselves. In some cases creating defenses against these attacks would have taken days.

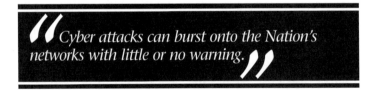

Cyber attacks can burst onto the Nation's networks with little or no warning.

A key lesson derived from these and other such cyber attacks is that organizations that rely on networked computer systems must take proactive steps to identify and remedy their vulnerabilities, rather than waiting for an attacker to be stopped or until alerted of an impending attack. Vulnerability assessment and remediation activities must be ongoing. An information technology security audit conducted by trained professionals to identify infrastructure vulnerabilities can take months. Subsequently, the process of creating a multi-layered defense and a resilient network to remedy the most serious vulnerabilities could take several additional months. The process must then be regularly repeated.

Security Risks at Five Levels

Managing threat and reducing vulnerability in cyberspace is a particularly complex challenge because of the number and range of different types of users. Cyberspace security requires action on multiple levels and by a diverse group of actors because literally hundreds of millions of devices are interconnected by a network of networks. The problem of cyberspace security can be best addressed on five levels.

Level 1, the Home User/Small Business. Though not a part of a critical infrastructure the computers of home users can become part of networks of remotely controlled machines that are then used to attack critical infrastructures. Undefended home and small business computers, particularly those using digital subscriber line (DSL) or cable connections, are vulnerable to attackers who can employ the use of those machines without the owner's knowledge. Groups of such "zombie" machines can then be used by third-party actors to launch denial-of-service (DoS) attacks on key Internet nodes and other important enterprises or critical infrastructures.

Level 2, Large Enterprises. Large-scale enterprises (corporations, government agencies, and universities) are common targets for cyber attacks. Many such enterprises are part of critical infrastructures. Enterprises require clearly articulated, active information security policies and programs to audit compliance with cybersecurity best practices. According to the U.S. intelligence community, American networks will be increasingly targeted by malicious actors both for the data and the power they possess.

Level 3, Critical Sectors/Infrastructures. When organizations in sectors of the economy, government, or academia unite to address common cybersecurity problems, they can often reduce the burden on individual enterprises. Such collaboration often produces shared institutions and mechanisms, which, in turn, could have cyber vulnerabilities whose exploitation could directly affect the operations of member enterprises and the sector as a whole. Enterprises can also reduce cyber risks by participating in groups that develop best practices, evaluate technological offerings, certify products and services, and share information.

Several sectors have formed Information Sharing and Analysis Centers (ISACs) to monitor for cyber attacks directed against their respective infrastructures. ISACs are also a vehicle for sharing information about attack trends, vulnerabilities, and best practices.

New [computer] vulnerabilities are created or discovered regularly.

Level 4, National Issues and Vulnerabilities. Some cybersecurity problems have national implications and cannot be solved by individual enterprises or infrastructure sectors alone. All sectors share the Internet. Accordingly, they are all at risk if its mechanisms (e.g., protocols and routers) are not secure. Weaknesses in widely used software and hardware products can also create problems at the national level, requiring coordinated activities for the research and development of improved technologies. Additionally, the lack of trained and certified cybersecurity professionals also merits national-level concern.

Level 5, Global. The worldwide web is a planetary information grid of systems. Internationally shared standards enable interoperability among the world's computer systems. This interconnectedness, however, also means that problems on one continent have the potential to affect computers on another. We therefore rely on international cooperation to share information related to cyber issues and, further, to prosecute cyber criminals. Without such cooperation, our collective ability to detect, deter, and minimize the effects of cyber-based attacks would be greatly diminished.

Need for Constant Vigilance

New vulnerabilities are created or discovered regularly. The process of securing networks and systems, therefore, must also be continuous. The Computer Emergency Response Team/Coordination Center (CERT/CC) notes that not only are the numbers of cyber incidents and attacks increasing at an alarming rate, so too are the numbers of vulnerabilities that an attacker could exploit. Identified computer security vulnerabilities—faults in software and hardware that could permit unauthorized network access or allow an attacker to cause network damage—increased significantly from 2000 to 2002, with the number of vulnerabilities going from 1,090 to 4,129.

The mere installation of a network security device is not a substitute for maintaining and updating a network's defenses. Ninety percent of the participants in a recent Computer Security Institute survey reported using antivirus software on their network systems, yet 85 percent of their systems had been damaged by computer viruses. In the same survey, 89 percent of the respondents had installed computer firewalls, and 60 percent had intrusion detection systems. Nevertheless, 90 percent reported that security breaches had taken place, and 40 percent of their systems had been penetrated from outside their network.

The majority of security vulnerabilities can be mitigated through good security practices. As these survey numbers indicate, however, practicing good security includes more than simply installing those devices. It also requires operating them correctly and keeping them current through regular patching and virus updates.

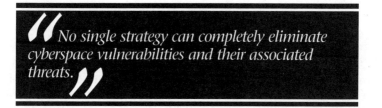

No single strategy can completely eliminate cyberspace vulnerabilities and their associated threats.

For individual companies and the national economy as a whole, improving computer security requires investing attention, time, and money. For fiscal year 2003, President Bush requested that Congress increase funds to secure federal computers by 64 percent. President Bush's investment in securing federal computer networks now will eventually reduce overall expenditures through cost-saving E-Government solutions, modern enterprise management, and by reducing the number of opportunities for waste and fraud.

For the national economy—particularly its information technology industry component—the dearth of trusted, reliable, secure information systems presents a barrier to future growth. Much of the potential for economic growth made possible by the information technology revolution has yet to be realized—deterred in part by cyberspace security risks. Cyberspace vulnerabilities place more than transactions at risk; they jeopardize intellectual property, business operations, infrastructure services, and consumer trust.

Conversely, cybersecurity investments result in more than costly overhead expenditures. They produce a return on investment. Surveys repeatedly show that:

- Although the likelihood of suffering a severe cyber attack is difficult to estimate, the costs associated with a successful one are likely to be greater than the investment in a cybersecurity program to prevent it; and
- Designing strong security protocols into the information systems architecture of an enterprise can reduce its overall operational costs by enabling cost-saving processes, such as remote access and customer or supply-chain interactions, which could not occur in networks lacking appropriate security.

These results suggest that, with greater awareness of the issues, companies can benefit from increasing their levels of cybersecurity. Greater awareness and voluntary efforts are critical components of the *National Strategy to Secure Cyberspace.*

Cooperating to Reduce Risk

Until recently overseas terrorist networks had caused limited damage in the United States. On September 11, 2001, that quickly changed. One estimate places the increase in cost to our economy from attacks to U.S. information systems at 400 percent over four years. While those losses remain relatively limited, that too could change abruptly.

Every day in the United States individual companies, and home computer users, suffer damage from cyber attacks that, to the victims represent significant losses. Conditions likewise exist for relative measures of damage to occur on a national level, affecting the networks and systems on which the Nation depends:

- Potential adversaries have the intent;
- Tools that support malicious activities are broadly available; and,
- Vulnerabilities of the Nation's systems are many and well known.

No single strategy completely eliminate cyberspace vulnerabilities and their associated threats. Nevertheless, the Nation must act to manage risk responsibly and to enhance its ability to minimize the damage that results from attacks that do occur. Through this statement, we reveal nothing to potential foes that they and others do not already know. In 1997 a Presidential Commission identified the risks in a seminal public report. In 2000 the first national plan to address the problem was published. Citing these risks, President Bush issued an Executive Order in 2001, making cybersecurity a priority, and accordingly, increasing funds to secure federal networks. In 2002 the President moved to consolidate and strengthen federal cybersecurity agencies as part of the proposed Department of Homeland Security.

Despite increased awareness around the importance of cybersecurity and the measures taken thus far to improve our capabilities, cyber risks continue to underlie our national information networks and the critical systems they manage. Reducing that risk requires an unprecedented, active partnership among diverse components of our country and our global partners.

The federal government could not—and, indeed, should not—secure the computer networks of privately owned banks, energy companies, transportation firms, and other parts of the private sector. The federal government should likewise not intrude into homes and small businesses, into universities, or state and local agencies and departments to create secure computer networks. Each American who depends on cyberspace, the network of information networks, must secure the part that they own or for which they are responsible.

7

Cyberterrorism Is Not a Major Threat

Joshua Green

Joshua Green is editor of the Washington Monthly *newsmagazine.*

Ever since the terrorist attacks of September 11, 2001, the Bush administration and other groups have repeatedly warned that terrorists might strike the nation's computer networks. However, these alarmists considerably exaggerate the risk of cyberterrorism. Terrorists can kill people, but not by means of computers. Computers controlling crucial assets such as nuclear weapons and airliners are much better protected against outside takeover than most people realize. Hackers might break into systems that control infrastructure such as electric power grids, oil pipelines, and dams, but causing actual damage to these targets requires specialized knowledge that terrorists are unlikely to possess.

Private agendas as well as ignorance fuel the hysteria about cyberterrorism. For example, technology companies eagerly exploit the ignorance of lawmakers and politicians about technology in order to sell their products. By exaggerating the dangers of cyberterrorism, the government creates more public anxiety about terrorism in general, which allows it to garner more support for its war on terror. Cybersecurity is a serious problem, but it is not one that involves terrorists.

Again and again since [the terrorist attacks of] September 11, President Bush, Vice President Cheney, and senior admin-

Joshua Green, "The Myth of Cyberterrorism," *Washington Monthly*, vol. 34, November 2002, pp. 8–13. Copyright © 2002 by Washington Monthly Publishing, LLC, 733 15th St. NW, Suite 520, Washington DC 20005. (202) 393-5155. Web site: www.washingtonmonthly.com. Reproduced by permission.

istration officials have alerted the public not only to the dangers of chemical, biological, and nuclear weapons but also to the further menace of cyberterrorism. "Terrorists can sit at one computer connected to one network and can create worldwide havoc," warned Homeland Security Director Tom Ridge in a representative observation last April [2002]. "[They] don't necessarily need a bomb or explosives to cripple a sector of the economy, or shut down a power grid."

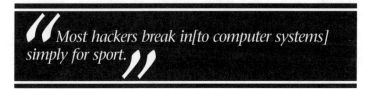

Most hackers break in[to computer systems] simply for sport.

Even before September 11, Bush was fervently depicting an America imminently in danger of an attack by cyberterrorists, warning during his presidential campaign that "American forces are overused and underfunded precisely when they are confronted by a host of new threats and challenges—the spread of weapons of mass destruction, the rise of cyberterrorism, the proliferation of missile technology." In other words, the country is confronted not just by the specter of terrorism, but by a menacing new breed of it that is technologically advanced, little understood, and difficult to defend against. Since September 11, these concerns have only multiplied. A survey of 725 cities conducted by the National League of Cities for the anniversary of the attacks shows that cyberterrorism ranks with biological and chemical weapons atop officials' lists of fears.

Concern over cyberterrorism is particularly acute in Washington. As is often the case with a new threat, an entire industry has arisen to grapple with its ramifications—think tanks have launched new projects and issued white papers, experts have testified to its dangers before Congress, private companies have hastily deployed security consultants and software designed to protect public and private targets, and the media have trumpeted the threat with such front-page headlines as this one, in *The Washington Post* last June [2002]: "Cyber-Attacks by Al Qaeda Feared, Terrorists at Threshold of Using Internet as Tool of Bloodshed, Experts Say."

The federal government has requested $4.5 billion for infrastructure security [in 2003]: the FBI boasts more than 1,000 "cyber investigators"; President Bush and Vice President Cheney

58

keep the issue before the public; and in response to September 11, Bush created the office of "cybersecurity czar" in the White House, naming to this position Richard Clarke, who has done more than anyone to raise awareness, including warning that "if an attack comes today with information warfare . . . it would be much, much worse than Pearl Harbor."

It's no surprise, then, that cyberterrorism now ranks alongside other weapons of mass destruction in the public consciousness. Americans have had a latent fear of catastrophic computer attack ever since a teenage Matthew Broderick hacked into the Pentagon's nuclear weapons system and nearly launched World War III in the 1983 movie *War Games.* Judging by official alarums and newspaper headlines, such scenarios are all the more likely in today's wired world.

There's just one problem: There is no such thing as cyberterrorism—no instance of anyone ever having been killed by a terrorist (or anyone else) using a computer. Nor is there compelling evidence that al Qaeda or any other terrorist organization has resorted to computers for any sort of serious destructive activity. What's more, outside of a Tom Clancy novel, computer security specialists believe it is virtually impossible to use the Internet to inflict death on a large scale, and many scoff at the notion that terrorists would bother trying. "I don't lie awake at night worrying about cyberattacks ruining my life," says Dorothy Denning, a computer science professor at Georgetown University and one of the country's foremost cybersecurity experts. "Not only does [cyberterrorism] not rank alongside chemical, biological, or nuclear weapons, but it is not anywhere near as serious as other potential physical threats like car bombs or suicide bombers."

Washington hypes cyberterrorism incessantly.

Which is not to say that cybersecurity isn't a serious problem—it's just not one that involves terrorists. Interviews with terrorism and computer security experts, and current and former government and military officials, yielded near unanimous agreement that the real danger is from the criminals and other hackers who did $15 billion in damage to the global economy [in 2001] using viruses, worms, and other readily available tools. That figure is sure to balloon if more isn't done to protect vulnerable computer systems, the vast majority of which are in the private sector. Yet when it comes to imposing the tough measures on business necessary to protect against the real cyberthreats, the Bush administration has balked.

Hollywood Scenarios

When ordinary people imagine cyberterrorism, they tend to think along Hollywood plot lines, doomsday scenarios in which terrorists hijack nuclear weapons, airliners, or military computers from halfway around the world. Given the colorful history of federal boon-doggles—billion-dollar weapons systems that misfire, $600 toilet seats—that's an understandable concern. But, with few exceptions, it's not one that applies to preparedness for a cyberattack. "The government is miles ahead of the private sector when it comes to cybersecurity," says Michael Cheek, director of intelligence for iDefense, a Virginia-based computer security company with government and private-sector clients. "Particularly the most sensitive military systems."

Serious effort and plain good fortune have combined to bring this about. Take nuclear weapons. The biggest fallacy about their vulnerability, promoted in action thrillers like *War Games*, is that they're designed for remote operation. "[The movie] is premised on the assumption that there's a modem bank hanging on the side of the computer that controls the missiles," says Martin Libicki, a defense analyst at the RAND Corporation. "I assure you, there isn't." Rather, nuclear weapons and other sensitive military systems enjoy the most basic form of Internet security: they're "air-gapped," meaning that they're not physically connected to the Internet and are therefore inaccessible to outside hackers. (Nuclear weapons also contain "permissive action links," mechanisms to prevent weapons from being armed without inputting codes carried by the president.) A retired military official was somewhat indignant at the mere suggestion: "As a general principle, we've been looking at this thing for 20 years. What cave have you been living in if you haven't considered this [threat]?"

When it comes to cyberthreats, the Defense Department has been particularly vigilant to protect key systems by isolating them from the Net and even from the Pentagon's internal network. All new software must be submitted to the National

Security Agency for security testing. "Terrorists could not gain control of our spacecraft, nuclear weapons, or any other type of high-consequence asset," says Air Force Chief Information Officer John Gilligan. [Since late 2001], Pentagon CIO [chief information officer] John Stenbit has enforced a moratorium on new wireless networks, which are often easy to hack into, as well as common wireless devices such as PDAs [personal digital assistants], BlackBerrys, and even wireless or infrared copiers and faxes.

The September 11 hijackings led to an outcry that airliners are particularly susceptible to cyberterrorism. Earlier this year [2002], for instance, Sen. Charles Schumer (D-N.Y.) described "the absolute havoc and devastation that would result if cyberterrorists suddenly shut down our air traffic control system, with thousands of planes in mid-flight." In fact, cybersecurity experts give some of their highest marks to the FAA [Federal Aviation Administration] which reasonably separates its administrative and air traffic control systems and strictly air-gaps the latter. And there's a reason the 9/11 hijackers used box-cutters instead of keyboards: It's impossible to hijack a plane remotely, which eliminates the possibility of a high-tech 9/11 scenario in which planes are used as weapons.

Another source of concern is terrorist infiltration of our intelligence agencies. But here, too, the risk is slim. The CIA's [Central Intelligence Agency's] classified computers are also air-gapped, as is the FBI's [Federal Bureau of Investigation's] entire computer system. "They've been paranoid about this forever," says Libicki, adding that paranoia is a sound governing principle when it comes to cybersecurity. Such concerns are manifesting themselves in broader policy terms as well. One notable characteristic of last year's [2001] Quadrennial Defense Review was how strongly it focused on protecting information systems.

But certain tics in the way government agencies procure technology have also—entirely by accident—helped to keep them largely free of hackers. For years, agencies eschewed off-the-shelf products and insisted instead on developing proprietary systems, unique to their branch of government—a particularly savvy form of bureaucratic self-preservation. When, say, the Department of Agriculture succeeded in convincing Congress that it needed a specially designed system, both the agency and the contractor benefited. The software company was assured the agency's long-term business, which became dependent on its product; in turn, bureaucrats developed an expertise with the software that made them difficult to replace. This, of course, fostered colossal inefficiencies—agencies often couldn't communicate with each other, minor companies developed fiefdoms in certain agencies, and if a purveyor went bankrupt, the agency was left with no one to manage its technology. But it did provide a peculiar sort of protection: Outside a select few, no one understood these specific systems well enough to violate them. So in a sense, the famous inability of agencies like the FBI and INS [Immigration and Naturalization Service] to share information because of incompatible computer systems has yielded the inadvertent benefit of shielding them from attack.

What About Infrastructure?

That leaves the less-protected secondary targets—power grids, oil pipelines, dams, and water systems that don't present opportunities as nightmarish as do nuclear weapons, but nonetheless seem capable, under the wrong hands, of causing their own mass destruction. Because most of these systems are in the private sector and are not yet regarded as national security loopholes, they tend to be less secure than government and military systems. In addition, companies increasingly use the Internet to manage such processes as oil-pipeline flow and water levels in dams by means of "supervisory control and data acquisition" systems, or SCADA, which confers remote access. Most experts see possible vulnerability here, and though terrorists have never attempted to exploit it, media accounts often sensationalize the likelihood that they will.

To illustrate the supposed ease with which our enemies could subvert a dam, *The Washington Post*'s June [2002] story on al Qaeda cyberterrorism related an anecdote about a 12-year-old who hacked into the SCADA system at Arizona's Theodore Roosevelt Dam in 1998, and was, the article intimated, within mere keystrokes of unleashing millions of gallons of water upon helpless downstream communities. But a subsequent investigation by the tech-news site CNet.com revealed the tale to be largely apocryphal—the incident occurred in 1994, the hacker was 27, and, most importantly, investigators concluded that he couldn't have gained control of the dam and that no lives or property were ever at risk.

Most hackers break in simply for sport. To the extent that these hacks occur, they're mainly Web site defacements, which are a nuisance, but leave the intruder no closer to exploiting the system in any deadly way. Security experts dismiss such hackers as "ankle biters" and roll their eyes at prognostications of doom.

Of course, it's conceivable that a computer-literate terrorist truly intent on wreaking havoc could hack into computers at a dam or power company. But once inside, it would be far more difficult for him to cause significant damage than most people realize. "It's not the difficulty of doing it," says RAND's Libicki. "It's the difficulty of doing it and having any real consequence." "No one explains precisely the how, whys, and wherefores of these apocalyptic scenarios," says George Smith, the editor of *Crypt Newsletter*, which covers computer security issues. "You always just get the assumption that chemical plants can be made to explode, that the water supply can be polluted—things that are even hard to do physically are suddenly assumed to be elementary because of the prominence of the Internet."

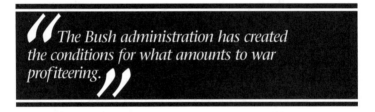

The Bush administration has created the conditions for what amounts to war profiteering.

Few besides a company's own employees possess the specific technical know-how required to run a specialized SCADA system. The most commonly cited example of SCADA exploitation bears this out. [In 2000], an Australian man used an Internet connection to release a million gallons of raw sewage along Queensland's Sunshine Coast after being turned down for a government job. When police arrested him, they discovered that he'd worked for the company that designed the sewage treatment plant's control software. This is true of most serious cybersecurity breaches—they tend to come from insiders. It was Robert Hanssen's [an FBI agent arrested for spying in February 2001] familiarity with the FBI's computer system that allowed him to exploit it despite its security. In both cases, the perpetrators weren't terrorists but rogue employees with specialized knowledge difficult, if not impossible, for outsiders to acquire— a security concern, but not one attributable to cyberterrorism.

Terrorists might, in theory, try to recruit insiders. But even if they succeeded, the degree of damage they could cause would still be limited. Most worst-case scenarios (particularly those put forth by government) presuppose that no human beings are keeping watch to intervene if something goes wrong. But especially in the case of electrical power grids, oil and gas utilities, and communications companies, this is simply untrue. Such systems get hit all the time by hurricanes, floods, or tornadoes, and company employees are well rehearsed in handling the fallout. This is equally true when the trouble stems from human action. In California [in 2000], energy companies like Enron and El Paso Corp. conspired to cause power shortages that led to brownouts and blackouts—the same effects cyberterrorists would wreak. As Smith points out, "There were no newspaper reports of people dying as a result of the blackouts. No one lost their mind." The state suffered only minor (if demoralizing) inconvenience.

But perhaps the best indicator of what is realistic came last July [2002] when the U.S. Naval War College contracted with a research group to simulate a massive attack on the nation's information infrastructure. Government hackers and security analysts gathered in Newport, R.I., for a war game dubbed "Digital Pearl Harbor." The result? The hackers failed to crash the Internet, though they did cause serious sporadic damage. But, according to a CNet.com report, officials concluded that terrorists hoping to stage such an attack "would require a syndicate with significant resources, including $200 million, country-level intelligence and five years of preparation time.". . .

Government Hype

Yet Washington hypes cyberterrorism incessantly "Cyberterrorism and cyberattacks are sexy right now. It's novel, original, it captures people's imagination," says Georgetown's Denning. Indeed, a peculiar sort of one-upmanship has developed when describing the severity of the threat. The most popular term, "electronic Pearl Harbor," was coined in 1991 by an alarmist tech writer named Winn Schwartau to hype a novel. For a while, in the mid-1990s, "electronic Chernobyl" was in vogue. Early [in 2002] Sen. Charles Schumer (D-N.Y.) warned of a looming "digital Armageddon." And the Center for Strategic and International Studies, a Washington think tank, has christened its own term, "digital Waterloo."

Why all this brooding over so relatively minor a threat? Ignorance is one reason. Cyberterrorism merges two spheres—

terrorism and technology—that most lawmakers and senior administration officials don't fully understand and therefore tend to fear, making them likelier to accede to any measure, if only out of self-preservation. Just as tellingly, many are eager to exploit this ignorance. Numerous technology companies, still reeling from the collapse of the tech bubble, have recast themselves as innovators crucial to national security and boosted their Washington presence in an effort to attract federal dollars. As Ohio State University law professor Peter Swire explained to *Mother Jones*, "Many companies that rode the dot-com boom need to find big new sources of income. One is direct sales to the federal government; another is federal mandates. If we have a big federal push for new security spending, that could prop up the sagging market."

But lately, a third motive has merged: Stoking fears of cyberterrorism helps maintain the level of public anxiety about terrorism generally, which in turn makes it easier for the administration to pass its agenda. . . .

Hiding the Real Threat

The danger of hyping a threat like cyberterrorism is that once the exaggeration becomes clear, the public will grow cynical toward warnings about real threats. The Chicken Little approach might be excusable were the Bush administration hyping cyberterrorism in order to build political momentum for dealing with the true problem posed by hackers and shoddy software. There is a precedent for this sort of thing. In the midst of all the anxiety about the Y2K bug, the federal government and the SEC [Securities and Exchange Commission] came up with a novel way to ensure that private companies were ready: They required businesses to disclose their preparations to shareholders, setting goals and letting market forces do the rest.

There were high hopes, then, for the Bush administration's National Strategy to Secure Cyberspace—the culmination of a year's effort to address the country's post-9/11 cybersecurity problems. Clarke's team circulated early drafts that contained what most experts considered to be solid measures for shoring up security in government, business, and home computers. But the business community got word that the plan contained tough (read: potentially costly) prescriptions, and petitioned the White House, which gutted them. When a draft of the plan was rolled out in mid-September 2002 Bill Conner, president of the computer security firm Entrust, told *The Washington Post*, "It looks as though a Ph.D. wrote the government items, but it reads like someone a year out of grade school wrote the rest of the plan."

It's hard to imagine a worse outcome for all involved, even private industry. By knuckling under to the business community's anti-regulatory impulses, Bush produced a weak plan that ultimately leaves the problem of cybersecurity to persist. It proposes no regulations, no legislation, and stops well short of even the Y2K approach, prompting most security experts to dismiss it out of hand. What it does do instead is continue the stream of officially sanctioned scaremongering about cyberattack, much to the delight of software companies IT [information technology] security remains one of the few bright spots in the depressed tech market and thus that important sector of the market is perfectly satisfied with the status quo. But as the Nimda virus proved, even companies that pay for security software (and oppose government standards) don't realize just how poorly it protects them. So in effect, the Bush administration has created the conditions for what amounts to war profiteering—frightening businesses into investing in security, but refusing to force the changes necessary to make software safe and effective.

The way the Bush White House has exaggerated the likelihood of cyberterrorism is familiar to anyone who's followed its style of government. This is an administration that will frequently proclaim a threat (the Saddam/al Qaeda connection, for instance) in order to forward its broader agenda, only to move on nonchalantly when evidence proves elusive or nonexistent. But in this case, by moving on, Bush leaves unaddressed something that really is a problem—just not one that suits the administration's interests. Forced to choose between increasing security and pleasing his business base, the president has chosen the latter. Hyping a threat that doesn't exist while shrinking from one that does is no way to protect the country.

8

Internet Use Increases the Risk of Identity Theft

Joseph Mann

Joseph Mann writes about international affairs for the Los Angeles Times, Financial Times, *and other publications.*

Thieves are increasingly using the Internet to obtain credit card numbers, Social Security numbers, and other private information that they can use to commit a variety of crimes, including making fraudulent purchases and opening fake credit card accounts. People's fear of becoming victim to such identity theft has made many reluctant to enter credit card numbers to make online purchases, causing concerns for the electronic commerce industry. Information brokers' databases have been hacked, and computers containing sensitive information have been stolen. "Phishing" e-mails trick people into entering their own personal data into fraudulent Web sites. Spyware, installed on personal computers without users' knowledge, captures passwords and identification numbers. Personal information can also be stolen in more traditional ways, but Internet theft may be more dangerous because people are often unaware that it has occurred until after the thieves have drained thousands of dollars from their bank accounts or credit cards.

ChoicePoint Inc. and LexisNexis[1] may face withering criticism for not keeping identity thieves out of their massive databases, but information brokers are far from the only sources of the Social Security numbers, addresses and other tidbits that fuel the fast-growing brand of fraud.

Just ask Brielle LaCosta, whose personal data was stolen when she responded to a seemingly official e-mail purportedly from online auctioneer EBay Inc. Within a few days of filling out the online forms, a car she had put up for auction had been sold out from under her and someone had run up $12,000 in charges on her credit card.

The rise of online commerce . . . has been a boon to [identity] thieves.

"I was stupid," said the 20-year-old college sophomore from Connecticut. "I put it all on there."

She's not the only one. Despite high-profile security breaches at big data aggregators like ChoicePoint and LexisNexis, online attacks, inside jobs and old-fashioned burglaries provide crooks the bulk of the personal data they need to open fake credit-card and other accounts.

Theft from Online Commerce

The rise of online commerce, in particular, has been a boon to thieves. Obtaining sensitive identifying information has become so easy, according to investigators, that the wholesale rate for valid credit-card numbers has fallen to as little as a dollar apiece.

"Consumers are not equipped to defend themselves properly," said Gartner Inc. data security analyst Avivah Litan. Among thieves' weapons of choice are so-called "phishing" attacks like the one that snared LaCosta, in which e-mailers pretend to be from a bank or other commerce site and refer people to sites that look official, and the use of spyware that surreptitiously logs account passwords as victims type.

1. information brokers who reported in early 2005 that hackers had invaded their databases of personal information

As those tools become more effective, "there's no lack of supply of stolen credit-card information," said former Assistant U.S. Attorney Scott Christie, who prosecuted members of Shadowcrew, an accused identity-theft ring. Some thieves try to obtain card numbers issued by banks in specific parts of the country, making fraudulent purchases less likely to stick out on consumers' bills because they look local.

So worried are people about attacks that the percentage of online shoppers willing to enter a credit-card number has flattened out after several years of sharp growth, sparking concern that electronic commerce may start to slow down.

"It took several years for e-commerce to take off," said Shawn Eldridge, chairmen of the Trusted Electronic Communications Forum. "Now the same problem is creeping up. The underlying trust people have in the Internet is being eroded again."

Inside Jobs

To be sure, identity theft is nothing new and plenty of information is swiped through tried-and-true methods that originated long before the rise of the Internet or data miners like ChoicePoint and LexisNexis. In many cases, the original leak of sensitive data comes from an employee inside a merchant or other company. A forthcoming study of 1,037 identity theft arrests found that more than 50% involve corporate insiders, said study co-author Judith Collins, a criminal justice professor at Michigan State University.

"The biggest problem is the workplace, and the biggest problem in the workplace is there's a lack of personnel security," Collins said.

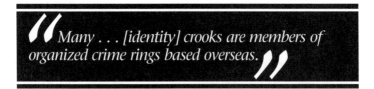

Many . . . [identity] crooks are members of organized crime rings based overseas.

In one instance, a contract employee at General Motors Corp. took information on thousands of company executives home from her last day of work. She was caught and convicted, but while still on probation, she was hired elsewhere and did the same thing, Collins said.

Robberies and burglaries trigger some identity thefts, giving criminals enough information to take out a loan in the victim's name or charge purchases to an existing credit card. Some restaurant and gasoline station workers run credit cards through unauthorized, special machines in order to copy the encoded information that can be used to make counterfeit cards. Big scores come from corporate databases or volume operations like spyware and phishing.

The ChoicePoint and LexisNexis thieves gained regular access to much broader files on ordinary citizens maintained by the two data giants. As is far more common, Shadowcrew got hold of card numbers and other information from hacked databases, prosecutor Christie said.

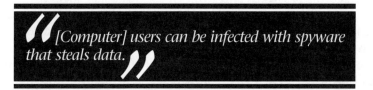

[Computer] users can be infected with spyware that steals data.

"Many online merchants have credit-card databases that are accessible online, which makes it very tempting for hackers who can get hundreds of thousands—or even millions—of numbers at one fell swoop," he said.

Thieves have rifled through the databases of such companies as BJ's Wholesale Club, CD Universe and Data Processors international, a credit-card handler with files on 8 million Master-Cards and Visas. In California, the biggest possible breach so far reported under the state's unique disclosure law came at UC [University of California] Berkeley, where a researcher had the Social Security numbers, names and dates of birth of more than 1 million people stored on a computer that was hacked.

Trade-group leaders and industry analysts say penalties are slight and enforcement has been weak, in part because many of the crooks are members of organized crime rings based overseas. The problem has been compounded, they say, because no single U.S. agency is in charge of investigating ID theft and related fraud. Cases are divided among local and state authorities, the Secret Service, the FBI and the many multi-agency task forces set up by geographic area.

The Trusted Electronic Communications Forum was founded last year [2004] by IBM Corp., Best Buy Co. and others to develop standards for combating phishing attacks with technology. Since then, the number of malicious e-mails has soared, more than doubling in the three months through January [2005].

Even longtime Internet users have been fooled by phishing pitches. Mark Nichols, a consignment store owner in Crosby, N.D., has been planning to update his credit-card information on his EBay account when an e-mail told him his account had been suspended. "I believed it because I knew that credit-card number I used needed to be updated. It took me to a site that looked OK," Nichols said.

After he entered his user name and password, Nichols wondered why his account page didn't appear. Returning to the original e-mail message, Nichols studied the link and realized it hadn't taken him to an official EBay site after all. Nichols quickly changed his password and avoided serious consequences.

As for Brielle LaCosta, she got the same bogus "account suspended" message as Nichols. She thought the information she was entering—including a bank card and code number and the password for her e-mail account—seemed excessive. But she really wanted to sell the Volkswagen Jetta she had just put up for bidding on EBay.

Two days later, she couldn't sign in to her EBay account. A friend checked and told her the Jetta was listed on EBay as sold.

LaCosta figured out that her incoming e-mail was being forwarded to an American Online account, and she struck up an instant-message conversation with the man who had bilked her.

The man said he was working in Italy for a group that paid for his and others' tuition in exchange for phishing financial information. That information, he said, went into a database that helped get false identities for illegal immigrants in the U.S.

The thief took $200 out of LaCosta's bank account and ran up $12,000 in credit-card charges. Merchants covered those, leaving as her biggest loss so far the more than $200 in EBay listing fees she was charged for fraudulent auctions held after she lost control of her account.

In later conversations with LaCosta, the con man took pity, warning her to cancel the cards and to disregard future e-mails asking for information. By then, she had come to the same conclusion. "I'm really skeptical of everything," LaCosta said.

The Hidden Eye of Spyware

Even if they don't click on the Web link, users can be infected with spyware that steals data.

"Absent any affirmative conduct on your part, your personal

financial information can be sucked out of your computer," said Christie, who recommends that consumers keep financial information off machines connected to the Internet.

A big problem with phishing is that people have no idea they've been phished.

Other experts advise computer users to avoid electronic banking, stick to established online merchants, eschew debit cards online, never click on e-mailed links, and install a firewall and at least one well-reviewed anti-spyware program like Ad-Aware or Spybot Search & Destroy. Users report fewer problems with alternative Web browsers and Apple Computer Inc. operating systems.

Credit-card holders should read their bills carefully and get copies of their credit reports at least annually, and some specialists say consumers should change which cards they use as often as every six months.

While they privately worry about the future of e-commerce, some major banks and credit-card associations continue to assure the public that their information is safe online.

Via USA, banker Wells Fargo & Co. and online payment firm CheckFree Corp., all of which profit from Internet banking, paid for one report on the topic that was released this year [2005]. The most startling finding by the study's author, Javelin Strategy and Research: "Although there has been much recent public concern over electronic methods of obtaining information, most thieves still obtain personal information through traditional channels rather than through the Internet."

Traditional Theft

The report said 72% of ID theft crimes occurred the old-fashioned way, such as via a pinched wallet or pilfered mail. Javelin advised consumers to do more online banking, not less, because those who bank online check their records more frequently and therefore tend to detect improper billing sooner.

The problem with the study's widely reported conclusion is that they may be misleading. Only 54% of the victims surveyed knew how their information leaked. So only 72% of those cases were believed to be traditional theft—or 39%.

Javelin founder James Van Dyke argued that the majority of unsolved cases were likely to be physical-world crimes. Federal Trade Commission Associate Director Lois Greisman disagreed with Javelin's conclusion.

"We have concerns with putting out, frankly, numbers like that," she said, adding that extrapolating from the 54% who knew what happened to them doesn't make sense. "I know if I've lost my purse. A big problem with phishing is that people have no idea they've been phished."

9

Internet Use Decreases the Risk of Identity Theft

Jack M. Germain

Jack M. Germain is a newspaper and magazine writer who also works as an editorial consultant.

Many media reports have portrayed the Internet as a hotbed of identity and credit card theft, but such claims have been exaggerated. On the contrary, a recent study suggests that banking and paying bills online can reduce the risk of identity theft by up to 18 percent. Most identity thieves gain the information they need by stealing paper bills and account statements from trash bins or mailboxes rather than by gathering it online. Online banking and bill paying not only deprive thieves of paper bills but allow users to monitor their accounts continuously rather than once a month. Because of these and other advantages, use of the Internet for banking and bill paying is growing in popularity.

James Van Dyke had a hunch [in 2003] that the commonly held belief that the Internet was causing an increase in identity theft and credit card fraud was not valid. Extensive research he conducted debunks many of the myths about the correlation between online activity and ID theft.

Contrary to popular opinion, Van Dyke, a research analyst for Javelin Strategy and Research, found that using the Internet for bill paying and banking can reduce risk by up to 18 percent and potentially save consumers up to 60 hours of personal time and US$1,100 in the cost of paper checks and postage.

His report, "Online Banking and Bill Paying: New Protection from Identity Theft," concludes that using the Internet can actually help protect consumers and businesses from two of the most common kinds of identity theft: fraudulent opening of new accounts and unauthorized use of existing accounts.

Van Dyke told TechNewsWorld that his research shows a correlation to the crime figures cited in the 2003 Federal Trade Commission annual report and United States Postal Service report. Those reports say more than 10 million Americans were victims of identity theft in 2002, and this crime cost businesses more than $47 billion. . . .

That amounts to a cost of $10,200 per victim for companies with such thefts and $1,180 per affected individual, Van Dyke said.

The popular view is that expanded use of the Internet by consumers is the chief cause of these growing crime figures. But Van Dyke said using the Internet for banking and paying bills actually reduces the threat of identity theft and banking fraud.

"That's because criminals get their information from traditional sources, such as low-tech, offline services," he said. "If consumers did more of their transactions online, they would actually reduce their risk of identity theft."

Van Dyke offers two examples from FTC statistics that support his view that doing business online is significantly safer. First, 14 percent of all new bank account cases resulting in fraud are traced to theft of paper from in front of victims' homes. Second, 5 percent of all identity theft could be reduced if paper billing were eliminated. He said paper billing creates a cost of $2.37 billion.

Go Online to Prevent Identity Theft

The average household receives 20 paper statements and bills per month, according to postal authorities. Criminals search through easily accessible trash and private mailboxes for bank and credit card information.

So a prime prevention strategy is for consumers to turn off the steady stream of paper billing and account summaries from vendors and banks they use. Many security advocates preach to consumers the need to switch to online billing whenever possible. When bills are provided online, vendors usually allow customers to pay those bills online as well.

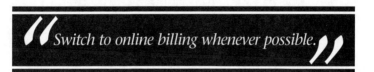

Switch to online billing whenever possible.

The problem develops when a vendor provides an online bill but does not let consumers turn off the monthly mailing of the statement. Shredding paper bills and credit card statements certainly reduces the threat of identity theft. But shredding doesn't prevent the possibility of document theft before consumers get their mail.

"By the time feeding paper into a shredder can happen, it is often too late. Vendors have to provide prevention upstream," Van Dyke told TechNewsWorld.

Detecting credit card and banking fraud goes hand-in-hand with preventing identity theft. According to financial-security experts, criminals turn to credit cards as their first method of finding victims.

It can take consumers between six and 36 days to view a mailed monthly account statement. That time delay drives a criminal's theft success. As security analysts put it, time is money to a criminal.

"There is a clear correlation between the time lag in seeing account statements and the detection of theft or unauthorized use," said Van Dyke.

The bottom line, he said, is that the Internet can help the consumer shut down abuses very quickly.

Check Bills and Statements Quickly

The most significant progress toward reducing consumer identity theft can be made by turning to online banking, as well as viewing and paying bills online. The Javelin report concluded that consumers who view online accounts and pay bills online are nearly four times more likely to actively monitor their vendor activity than those who wait for paper bills and monthly statements. That consumer-level watchfulness can be more effective in protecting against account fraud and identity theft than the millions of dollars businesses spend on fraud-monitoring technology.

The report also credits consumers with catching unauthorized account activity in more than 50 percent of all cases. This earlier detection can reduce consumer identity theft by 18 percent, according to experts.

Other industry watchers agree that online banking and bill payment are gaining strong footholds among consumers. A report issued in the first quarter of 2003 by the Yankee Group showed that Internet and credit card services get the highest use by consumers who review and pay their bills online.

"Since users of Internet service are already online, reviewing bills is a natural extension of the service. Additionally, credit card and long-distance service providers have been pushing electronic bill-paying and presentment (EBPP) longer than service providers in other verticals," wrote Lisa Cebollero, a Yankee Group billing and payment application strategies analyst, in the Yankee Group report. She added that existing Internet use has resulted in more visibility of online bill presentment and bill-paying options in other Internet service areas.

Javelin's Van Dyke said he is sure that careful use of the Internet by consumers will continue to reduce incidents of identity theft and transaction fraud. He added that many more people than ever before—with less education and technical savvy—are safely using the Internet to handle their banking and bill-paying tasks, and he expects to see that trend continue.

10

Cyberstalking Is Not Taken Seriously Enough

Deborah Radcliff

Deborah Radcliff is a journalist who writes about information security and the computer industry.

The experience of the staff members of a Lexington, Kentucky, newspaper, who were harassed both online and offline after firing a photographer, provides an example of the frustrations that victims of cyberstalking can face. Law enforcement officials often seem to be unable or unwilling to do anything about cyberstalking, or the use of computers to track, threaten, or harass individuals or companies. Since laws against cyberstalking are often weak and confusing, companies must provide their own protection against this crime. If a cyberstalker attacks them, they should keep a log of all the instances of harassment. They should use any means possible to identify the stalker, including hiring a private detective if necessary. Once a stalker is identified, either a civil suit or criminal prosecution may be possible, but companies that pursue such approaches may not be able to persuade police or district attorneys to cooperate with their efforts.

Shortly after she fired a freelance photographer for downloading pornography [in 1997] a vice president at the *Lexington Herald Leader* newspaper started getting strange phone calls from men who said they had met her in chat rooms and wanted to meet her in person.

Deborah Radcliff, "A Case of Cyberstalking," *Network World*, May 29, 2000, p. 56. Copyright © 2000 by Network World, Inc. Reproduced by permission of Reprint Management Services.

Then came subscriptions to *Playboy, Penthouse, Playgirl, Bride* and *Seventeen* magazines, none of which she ordered. A male executive who was also involved in firing the photographer started getting calls from females who thought they'd met him in chat rooms he never visited.

The publisher of the Knight-Ridder newspaper in Lexington, Ky., began receiving porn spam. In the most outrageous twist, Jones Fish in Williamsburg, Ky., called the vice president to discuss her order to stock a five-acre lake with fish. Of course, she knew nothing about the order.

At that point, the newspaper managers thought it would be a fairly simple matter to report the incidents to the police and have the man arrested. Unfortunately, three years have passed, the harassment continues [in 2000] and authorities are apparently powerless to do anything about it.

Companies Must Protect Themselves

With cyberstalking on the rise, the *Herald Leader* case provides a useful lesson for any network security executive who may run into a similar problem. When the incidents first began, the *Herald Leader* hired private detectives to track the activity back to the photographer. *Herald Leader* management pleaded with the postal inspector and the telephone company, contacted local and state police, and even the FBI, according to a high-ranking executive at the paper who asked not to be identified.

Under most state laws, this activity qualifies as stalking, which is usually a misdemeanor that law enforcement officials typically won't bother with unless there are more serious crimes or threat of bodily harm involved.

The harassment continues . . . and authorities are apparently powerless to do anything about it.

Because of these light penalties and the confusing, immature nature of state laws on cyberstalking, these cases are difficult to prosecute, says Lt. Commander Chris Malinowski, who heads the New York City Police Department's computer crime unit.

So what's a company to do if cyberstalking hits close to

home? "You have to attack things like this in phases," says Paul French, computer forensics lab manager for New Technologies, Inc., a training firm in Gresham, Ore. "First you find out who did it. Then get legal advice. And if you can't get it stopped, file a civil suit."

Sometimes just a call to the perpetrator may be enough to stop the stalking.

This is the procedure followed by Greggory Peck, a senior IT [information technology] security analyst at a Fortune 500 company, when he stumbles across cyberstalking cases among his employers. He gets involved in such cases an average of three times per year, he says. "This happens in almost every company I work for," he says. "People call me and say, 'I'm getting these very obscene e-mails.' The person doesn't know who it's from."

Stalking a Stalker

Peck starts by logging every event, just as the *Herald Leader* did. Then he retraces the cybersteps of the perpetrator. Companies that lack the skill to do this should look for a private detective who's well-versed in Internet evidence gathering, suggests Peck.

E-mail is the easiest to track by reading header information, following it back to the ISP [Internet service provider] and enlisting or subpoenaing the ISP to match evidence with its customer information. To do this, the ISP must compare its logs for connections that coincide with the dates and times the mails were sent to the victim.

In the case of a chat room scenario, in which the attacker pretends to be someone he's not, tracking is a little more difficult because the person calling or mailing the victim has also been duped by the perpetrator who leaves no obvious IP [Internet Protocol] address trail. But even this can be overcome with the help of the ISP.

"As a security analyst, the closest I've dealt with is someone using chat rooms to libel our company on a public message board," Peck says. "But we do have the ability, through Olittle brother 'probes and proxy servers, to see who went to chat at Yahoo.com at such and such time on Nov. 9, 1998,' he says.

"Then we could have used a subpoena to ask whose IP address this post originated from."

Enlisting Law Enforcement

The next step is to get an attorney with some cybersmarts to help determine whether to seek criminal charges, file a civil suit or neither, advises Alan Wernick, a partner in the Chicago office and co-chairman of McBride Baker & Coles' intellectual property law department. "Civil suits are one possible remedy," Wernick says. "If the cyberstalker is tying up company computer resources, then other issues may arise, like denial of use."

In that case, you're looking at a violation of the Computer Crime Act, which federal officials are obliged to look into. So if you want the help of law enforcement, look for activity like fraud or computer crime, or threat of bodily harm, Malinowski suggests.

For the most part, French and Peck follow the civil path because they, like the *Herald Leader*, can't find law enforcement officers to help them. And, Peck says, sometimes just a call to the perpetrator may be enough to stop the stalking. He says this is especially effective when you tell the harasser, "We know who you are. We know where you live. And we know what you're doing."

Just remember that if you're filing damages in a civil suit, most perpetrators don't have much to lose, Malinowski says. If you know the perpetrator's whereabouts, he advises to instead contact the prosecutor in the perpetrator's jurisdiction. State prosecutors, he says, are currently organizing and gearing up to deal with new cyberstalking laws coming out on a state-by-state basis. And when you do contact the prosecutor, bring logs and evidence that point to the perpetrator, Malinowski says.

Unfortunately, following this process doesn't guarantee results. The *Herald Leader* case shows just how difficult it is to stop a cyberstalker, let alone prosecute one.

"We've tracked the IP address to the perpetrator's computer two times. We've gone to the county attorney's office and they won't touch this," says a *Herald Leader* executive who asked not to be identified. "We've gone to the Lexington Police Department, the state police, even the FBI. Our publisher has spent a lot of time trying to keep law enforcement interested. What else can we do to get this stopped?"

11

Cyberstalking Is Taken Too Seriously

Lewis Z. Koch

Lewis Z. Koch is an investigative reporter.

The media would be less likely to publish hysterical stories about cyberstalking if they checked their facts more carefully. Internet-related crimes do occur, but claims about the growing prevalence of cyberstalking have been greatly exaggerated. Reporters in need of sensational stories, politicians courting votes for reelection, "experts" looking to bolster their own reputations, and activists in search of profitable agendas all contribute to the hype. Cyberstalking is in fact a quite rare crime. Unclear definitions of cyberstalking, as well as dubious extrapolations from academic studies that often were not intended to focus on the subject at all, have made this crime seem more common than it really is.

"Common sense and some growing anecdotal evidence would tell you that cyberstalking is a growing problem," said Associate Deputy Attorney General John Bentivoglio, who handles cybercrime and cyberstalking issues at the Department of Justice. That's when alarm bells went off in my head.

More than three decades ago on my third day as a cub reporter at Chicago's City News Bureau, a hulking, menacing, slovenly city editor named Arnold Dornfeld lumbered up to me and asked, "Does your mother love ya, chum?"

"Yes," I responded eagerly.

"How d'ya know?"

I coughed nervously and mumbled, "Of course she does."

"Call her and check." I looked for a smile on his face. There was none. Then he leaned in and said, "Call her or you're fired."

I quickly dialed my mother, asked the question, got a positive reply, hung up and looked at Dornfeld. "She said she loves me."

Dornfeld looked deep into my eyes and said, without a shred of humor, "Now you know."

Would that Bentivoglio had deigned to "call and check."

Distortions by the "Iron Quadrangle"

Is cyberstalking a plague, an international menace or a rare crime?

There are problems on the Internet—some real, others minuscule, many imaginary. There are criminal financial dealings on the Net, child porn and child molesters, dope dealers and terrorists. It's like life—real and, at times, grim, ugly and desperate.

But when it comes to cyberstalking, there's little justification for the hysteria.

When it comes to cyberstalking, there's little justification for the hysteria.

Joel Best, chairman of the Department of Sociology at the University of Delaware (www.udel.edu), in his brilliant, impeccably researched and highly readable book *Random Violence: How We Talk About New Crimes and New Victims*, had the sense to check out the stalking situation and found it to be wildly overblown.

The news media, in Best's analysis, is perpetually in need of new, attention-grabbing stories, a new crime wave or menace. This style of journalism, Best said, forms just one side of what he called an "iron quadrangle":

Side 1—Sensation mongers. Frenzy and melodrama are the very stuff of life for reporters and editors. They sell newspapers and magazines, drive TV ratings higher and alarm the public.

Side 2—Pandering politicians. Elected officials hold public hearings and give "outraged" speeches and interviews, call for new legislation that, of course, justifies their salaries and their re-election. Bureaucrats churn out reports like beavers building a dam.

Side 3—Trendy academics/experts/ problem solvers. The existence of "problems" opens the door to academics who need to "study" the problems over time. Meanwhile, quotable "experts and problem solvers" call for budget and personnel increases to combat the problems defined by the academics.

Side 4—Activists in search of a new agenda. There is an almost unlimited number of potential Internet addicts/victims, all of whom need care. Activists and professional advocates make themselves available to the new marketplace of victims.

This iron quadrangle has already taken real life hostage. Next stop: the Internet.

Doubtful Statistics

A perfect example of the iron quadrangle at work is the assessment of cyberstalking. How serious is it? The alleged number of stalkers in the U.S. is 200,000. That number has been floating around [since 1992]. The reporter who first reported it in 1992 can't exactly recall his source. Oprah Winfrey and Sally Jessy Raphael picked it up that year. California, with one actual stalking murder case, passed its antistalking law in 1992. Twenty-nine other states quickly followed with similar laws that year. Eighteen more states and the District of Columbia followed in 1993, triggered, it appears, by exactly two other stalking death cases in the nation.

> *[Researcher] Joel Best . . . had the sense to check out the stalking situation and found it to be wildly overblown.*

Three cases in all. Tragic, yes—but three cases in a nation of 270 million people. Yet activists immediately equated stalking with "violence against women/domestic violence," which allowed for plague-sized numbers. That is how a group called CyberAngels (www.cyberangels.org) came up with the numbers of 63,000 Internet stalkers and 474,000 victims worldwide, numbers even Bentivoglio's 1999 *Report on Cyberstalking: A New Chal-*

lenge for Law Enforcement and Industry warned in a footnote were "statistics from unspecified sources." How many specific cyberstalking cases does Bentivoglio's report cite? Six.

I asked Bentivoglio, if the data gathered from the stalking survey proved wrong, wouldn't his report's extrapolation of the extent of the problem be wrong as well. "Sure," he allowed.

A Misleading Study

Although the report is replete with words such as "trends" and "evidence," there is little factual support. Everything rests on a single study. The report describes it as a "large study on sexual victimization of college women, by researchers at the University of Cincinnati." It was a national telephone survey of 4,446 randomly selected women attending two- and four-year institutions of higher education.

As defined by the study, a stalking incident was anytime someone answered "yes" to the question: Has someone "repeatedly followed you, watched you, phoned, written, e-mailed or communicated with you in other ways that seemed obsessive and made you afraid or concerned for your safety." A veritable fruit salad of offenses and a wide range of reactions, but, hey, let's leave that aside.

The study claims that of the 13.1 percent who said they were stalked, "24.7 percent of the stalking incidents involved e-mail." In effect, Bentivoglio concluded, "25 percent of stalking incidents among college women could be classified as involving cyberstalking."

Only it's not true, at least according to one of the study's authors—Francis T. Cullen, research professor at the University of Cincinnati (www.uc.edu), the highly regarded past editor of *Justice Quarterly* and the *Journal of Crime and Justice*, and the former president of the Academy of Criminal Justice Sciences (www.acjs.org).

Cullen dismissed the cyber side of the stalking study, noting it only included a "couple of questions" related to the "cyberstalking area," and those questions were "not detailed." Cullen said that of those "couple of questions," no samples of threatening e-mail had been obtained, the questions were on a "general level," the study was "not a study of cyberstalking per se" and, "unfortunately," the research was conducted at such a level that, "other than knowing something had occurred, we actually don't know much about it."

What we're left with is a suspicious statistical extrapolation and a nearly nonexistent, shockingly weak study of cyberstalking that wasn't even a study of cyberstalking in the first place. If a reporter had handed Dornfeld this report, he would have torn it up, tossed it back and said, "Check it out, chum—and next time, come back with facts."

12

Internet Threats to Children Are Increasing

U.S. Department of Justice, Office for Victims of Crime

The Office for Victims of Crime is part of the U.S. Department of Justice. Established by the Victims of Crime Act in 1984, it oversees a variety of programs that help the victims of crime.

The Internet has made it easier for adults to commit crimes against children. Predators no longer have to look for potential victims in public places such as schoolyards, where they themselves might be spotted. Instead, they can disguise their identity online, pretending to be children or teens. In this guise, predators entice children to meet them to engage in sexual acts. Criminals also use the Internet to expose youth to child pornography. Growing computer use among young people puts more and more of them at risk for such victimization. The results of a 1999 survey that assessed the frequency of four types of online crimes against children confirm that the Internet can be a dangerous place for young people. Prosecuting cases of Internet-related crimes against children is complex because the cases are usually multijurisdictional, which makes investigations difficult. New legal approaches need to be developed to protect children from further victimization.

The growth of technology has changed our lives dramatically. Computers were viewed as a luxury or even an extravagance 30 years ago. We relied on television, newspapers, and radio as

U.S. Department of Justice, Office for Victims of Crime, "Internet Crimes Against Children," *OVC Bulletin*, December 2001, pp. 1–8.

primary sources of news and information. Cables, modems, and online services were virtually nonexistent.

Today, computers are prevalent in businesses, homes, schools, libraries, and even airports. The World Wide Web provides instant access to news, reference information, shopping, banking, stock trading, auctions, and travel information and reservations. People routinely use the Internet to take college courses, play games, listen to music, and view videos. Chat rooms and e-mails are now replacing telephones as our favorite means of long-distance communication.

Computers and the Internet have made the predator's job easier.

The proliferation of computer technology obviously has enhanced our lives in many ways, such as enabling improved productivity and efficiency at work, school, and home. Anyone with access to a computer and modem now has unparalleled recreational and educational opportunities.

Unfortunately, criminals are also using modern technology—to prey on innocent victims. Computers and the Internet have made the predator's job easier. Historically, child predators found their victims in public places where children tend to gather—schoolyards, playgrounds, and shopping malls. Today, with so many children online, the Internet provides predators a new place—cyberspace—to target children for criminal acts. This approach eliminates many of the risks predators face when making contact in person.

Who Is Vulnerable?

The sheer number of young people using computers today makes our concern for them well founded. Recent years have seen a great increase in access to and use of the Internet. By the end of 1998, more than 40 percent of all American homes had computers, and 25 percent had Internet access. This trend is expected to continue. Children and teenagers are one of the fastest growing groups of Internet users. An estimated 10 million kids are online today. By the year 2002, this figure is expected to increase to 45 million, and by 2005 to 77 million. With so many youth online and vulnerable to predators, it is extremely important for parents, law enforcement officials, prosecutors, and victim service providers to know as much as possible about Internet crimes against children so they can prevent victimization and prosecute offenders.

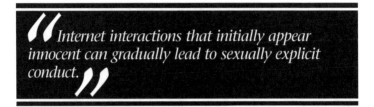

Internet interactions that initially appear innocent can gradually lead to sexually explicit conduct.

Traditionally, both intrafamilial offenders and strangers have found that young children and teenagers are perfect targets for criminal acts because they are often trusting, naive, curious, adventuresome, and eager for attention and affection. However, the most attractive factor to predators is that children and teenagers historically have not been viewed as credible witnesses. Today, the danger to children is even greater because the Internet provides predators anonymity. Whether the victimization occurs in person or over the Internet, the process is the same—the perpetrator uses information to target a child victim. For example, the predator may initiate an online friendship with a young person, sharing hobbies and interests. This may lead to the exchange of gifts and pictures. Just like the traditional predator who targets children in person, the online predator usually is willing to spend considerable time befriending and grooming a child. The predator wants to build the child's trust, which will allow the predator to get what he or she ultimately wants from the child.

Although no family is immune to the possibility that their child may be exploited and harassed on the Internet, a few factors make some children more vulnerable than others. Older children tend to be at greater risk because they often use the computer unsupervised and are more likely to engage in online discussions of a personal nature. Some victims become unwitting participants as they actively participate in chat rooms, trade e-mail messages, and send pictures online. Troubled or rebellious teens who are seeking emancipation from parental authority can be susceptible to Internet predators. The risk of victimization is greater for emotionally vulnerable youth who may be dealing with issues of sexual identity. These young people may be willing to engage in conversation that is both titillating and exciting but appears innocent and harmless. Unfortunately, Internet interactions that initially appear innocent can gradually lead to sexually explicit conduct.

Cybercrimes Affecting Children

Internet crimes are often thought of as victimless. Nothing could be further from the truth. Children and teenagers can and do become victims of Internet crimes. Predators contact teenagers and children over the Internet and victimize them by
- Enticing them through online contact for the purpose of engaging them in sexual acts.
- Using the Internet for the production, manufacture, and distribution of child pornography.
- Using the Internet to expose youth to child pornography and encourage them to exchange pornography.
- Enticing and exploiting children for the purpose of sexual tourism (travel with the intent to engage in sexual behavior) for commercial gain and/or personal gratification.

Several characteristics distinguish Internet crimes from other crimes committed against children:

Physical contact between the child and the perpetrator does not need to occur for a child to become a victim or for a crime to be committed. Innocent pictures or images of children can be digitally transformed into pornographic material and distributed across the Internet without the victims' knowledge.

The Internet provides a source for repeated, long-term victimization of a child that can last for years, often without the victim's knowledge. Once a child's picture is displayed on the Internet, it can remain there forever. Images can stay on the Internet indefinitely without damage to the quality of the image.

> *Although the Internet is a wonderfully fun and educational tool, it can also be very dangerous.*

These crimes transcend jurisdictional boundaries, often involving multiple victims from different communities, states, and countries. The geographic location of a child is not a primary concern for perpetrators who target victims over the Internet. Often, perpetrators travel hundreds of miles to different states and countries to engage in sexual acts with children they met over the Internet. Many of these cases involve local, state, federal, and international law enforcement entities in multiple jurisdictions.

Many victims of Internet crimes do not disclose their victimization or even realize that they have been victims of a crime. Whereas children who experience physical or sexual abuse may disclose the abuse to a friend, teacher, or parent, many victims of Internet crimes remain anonymous until pictures or images are discovered by law enforcement during an investigation. The presumed anonymity of Internet activities often provides a false sense of security and secrecy for both the perpetrator and the victim.

Youth Internet Safety Survey

Although it was clear that young people are using the Internet in ever-increasing numbers, no research existed on how many youth encounter unwanted sexual solicitations and exposure to sexual material and harassment online. To obtain a clearer picture of the scope of the problem, the National Center for Missing & Exploited Children (NCMEC) provided funding to Dr. David Finkelhor, Director of the Crimes Against Children Research Center at the University of New Hampshire, to conduct a research survey in 1999 on Internet victimization of youth. His research provides the best profile of this problem to date.

Crimes Against Children Research Center staff interviewed a nationally representative sample of 1,501 youth, aged 10 to 17, who used the Internet regularly. "Regular use" was defined as using the Internet at least once a month for the past 6 months on a computer at home, at school, in a library, at someone else's home, or in some other place.

The survey looked at four types of online victimization of youth, which Finkelhor defined as

- Sexual solicitation and approaches: Requests to engage in sexual activities or sexual talk or to give personal sexual information that were unwanted or, whether wanted or not, made by an adult.
- Aggressive sexual solicitation: Sexual solicitations involving offline contact with the perpetrator through mail, by telephone, or in person, or attempts or requests for offline contact.

- Unwanted exposure to sexual material: When online, opening e-mail, or opening e-mail links, and not seeking or expecting sexual material, being exposed to pictures of naked people or people having sex.
- Harassment: Threats or other offensive content (not sexual solicitation) sent online to the youth or posted online for others to see.

The survey also explored Internet safety practices used by youth and their families, what factors may put some youth more at risk for victimization than others, and the families' knowledge of how to report online solicitations and harassment.

What the Survey Found

The survey results offered the following statistical highlights:
- One in 5 youth received a sexual approach or solicitation over the Internet in the past year.
- One in 33 youth received an aggressive sexual solicitation in the past year. This means a predator asked a young person to meet somewhere, called a young person on the phone, and/or sent the young person correspondence, money, or gifts through the U.S. Postal Service.
- One in 4 youth had an unwanted exposure in the past year to pictures of naked people or people having sex.
- One in 17 youth was threatened or harassed in the past year.
- Most young people who reported these incidents were not very disturbed about them, but a few found them distressing.
- Only a fraction of all episodes was reported to authorities such as the police, an Internet service provider, or a hotline.
- About 25 percent of the youth who encountered a sexual approach or solicitation told a parent. Almost 40 percent of those reporting an unwanted exposure to sexual material told a parent.
- Only 17 percent of youth and 11 percent of parents could name a specific authority, such as the Federal Bureau of Investigation (FBI), CyberTipline, or an Internet service provider, to which they could report an Internet crime, although more indicated they were vaguely aware of such authorities.
- In households with home Internet access, one-third of

parents said they had filtering or blocking software on their computers.

The survey results confirm what is already known: although the Internet is a wonderfully fun and educational tool, it can also be very dangerous. According to the survey, one in five youth who regularly use the Internet received sexual solicitations or approaches during a 1-year period. The survey also found that offenses and offenders are more diverse than previously thought. In addition to pedophiles, other predators use the Internet. Nearly half (48 percent) of the offenders were other youth, and one-fourth of the aggressive episodes were initiated by females. Further, 77 percent of targeted youth were age 14 or older—not an age characteristically targeted by pedophiles. Although the youth stopped most solicitations by leaving the Web site, logging off, or blocking the sender, the survey confirmed current thinking that some youth are particularly vulnerable to online advances.

Cases involving Internet crimes against children are complex and labor intensive.

Most youth reported not being distressed by sexual exposures online. However, a significant 23 percent reported being very or extremely upset, 20 percent reported being very or extremely embarrassed, and 20 percent reported at least one symptom of stress. These findings point to the need for more research on the effects on youth of unwanted exposure to sexual materials and the indicators of potentially exploitative adult-youth relationships.

The large number of solicitations that went unreported by youth and families was of particular interest. This underreporting is attributed to feelings of embarrassment or guilt, ignorance that the incident was a reportable act, ignorance of how to report it, and perhaps resignation to a certain level of inappropriate behavior in the world.

Possibly due to the nature and small sample size of the survey, there were no reported incidences of traveler cases. The survey also revealed no incidences of completed Internet seduction or sexual exploitation, including trafficking of child pornography. Despite the findings of this survey, law enforcement agencies report increasing incidents of Internet crimes against children.

Challenges to Law Enforcement

Among the many findings of Finkelhor's survey, the most significant is that we are only beginning to realize the extent of the complex and increasingly prevalent phenomenon of Internet-based crimes against children. We have much to learn about the magnitude of the problem, the characteristics of its victims and perpetrators, its impact on children, and strategies for prevention and intervention. . . .

The future holds many challenges for those fighting Internet crimes against young people. Cases involving Internet crimes against children are complex and labor intensive for both the police and prosecutors. The time between victimization and arrest can be lengthy. These cases are usually multijurisdictional, which presents challenges in the investigation and prosecution of a case and can present problems for the criminal justice system, the child victim, and the family in terms of resources, travel, and court appearances.

Child victimization on the Internet is a complex matter. The full impact of such victimization on children is not completely understood. Family dynamics often play a significant role in children's denial of a crime and their willingness to participate in the investigation and prosecution. A child's ability to acknowledge and accept the crime can be linked to family values, peer pressure, and feelings of guilt, shame, and embarrassment. Denial and recantation can be common among children who unwittingly participated in the crime. Because of these issues, the greatest challenges facing law enforcement and victim service professionals are to identify the victims, protect their privacy, and serve them without further victimization.

Until more knowledge is gathered about Internet crime and its effects on victims, law enforcement and victim service professionals will continue working on Internet child exploitation using the tactics and standard approaches that have proved effective for working with other types of child victims.

Glossary

algorithm: The plan for the instructions that a computer will use to solve a problem or perform a task.

back door: A program or piece of code inserted by a computer virus that will allow a hacker to gain access to the computer at a later time.

BlackBerry: A model of the small, handheld computers, often called PDAs (personal digital assistants), that allow people to keep track of schedules, addresses, and other personal information.

boot sector: The portion of a computer's hard disk or an inserted diskette or CD that contains a program necessary for loading the computer's operating system into its random-access memory so that the computer can begin its normal functions.

broadband: A type of Internet connection (such as cable or DSL) that allows large amounts of information to be transferred to or from a computer quickly. It is especially useful for multimedia presentations (those that include sound and video).

browser (or Web browser): A program that allows a computer to display Web pages and access files on the Internet.

cable modem: A device that connects a computer to a cable TV service, allowing faster downloading of information from the Internet.

chat room: An interactive discussion on a particular topic, held on the Internet or through an online service, in which users type in messages on their computers and other users read the messages and respond immediately.

cracker: A term used by some to refer to a computer hacker who commits crimes.

denial-of-service attack: A form of computer vandalism in which a hacker sends large numbers of requests to a Web site within a short period. Because each of these messages must be acknowledged, the computer hosting the Web site becomes overloaded, causing the site to shut down temporarily. If the site belongs to a large company, the company can suffer considerable financial damage from business lost during the time the site is down.

DSL (digital subscriber line): A technology that considerably increases the speed at which digital information can be transferred through a telephone line.

ethical hacker: A hacker who is hired by businesses to reveal computer security flaws so that the flaws can be repaired.

executable file: A file containing a program that is ready to run on a particular computer.

exploit: A loophole that allows unauthorized entry into a computer system, or a program or technique that takes advantage of such a loophole.

firewall: A program or hardware device that monitors Internet transmissions to prevent unauthorized access to a computer network.

IP (Internet protocol) address: A unique number identifying a computer on the Internet. These numbers can be used to trace the source of e-mail messages or other activities.

IRC (Internet relay chat) channel: A service through which computer conferencing on the Internet takes place. Each channel is devoted to a particular subject. When a person joins a channel, the person's messages are broadcast to everyone logged into that channel.

ISP (Internet service provider): An organization that provides access to the Internet, usually for a monthly fee. For an additional fee, some ISPs also allow users to upload Web sites onto the Internet (the ISPs are said to "host" the sites).

IT (information technology): The technology of processing information by computer. Most large companies have officers or even whole departments devoted to IT.

listserv: An e-mail mailing list. A message posted to the listserv automatically goes to everyone on the list.

logic bomb: A hidden program that "triggers" an action, such as destroying data, when a certain time or condition is reached.

macro: A series of menu selections, keystrokes, or commands that are recorded and assigned a name or a key combination. Macros are used to automate often-repeated tasks, such as typing an address. Hackers sometimes attach destructive macros to word processing documents or e-mail messages.

PDA (personal digital assistant): A handheld computer that organizes personal information, such as a schedule, list of tasks to be done, or address book. Information is entered into a PDA with a special pen or stylus or a tiny keyboard. PDAs can also transmit information to and from desktop computers. The BlackBerry is a popular model of PDA.

phishing: An activity in which a criminal sends e-mail messages purporting to be from a trusted organization such as a bank. The messages request personal data such as Social Security numbers. Information obtained in this way is usually used for identity theft or other illicit purposes.

phone phreak: Someone who manipulates telephone technology for unauthorized or illegal purposes, such as making free long-distance calls.

protocol: Rules governing the transmitting and receiving of data over a network such as the Internet.

proxy or proxy server: A program that allows computers in a network to share an Internet connection and a single IP address. Proxies that allow access from outside the network (open proxies) are a security threat.

relay: A connection between a computer and an e-mail server.

router: A device that forwards packets of data from one computer network to another. Routers are often used to connect home or office networks to the Internet.

SAP system: An integrated database that provides business functions such as purchasing or accounting.

script kiddies: Inexperienced, often young, hackers who use existing hacking programs rather than creating their own. Veteran hackers usually look down on them.

server: A program that provides services such as e-mail or access to Web sites. Also, a computer in a network that is shared by multiple users, or software that allows such sharing.

social engineering: Hacker term for tricking people into providing information or services, for example, pretending to be a fellow employee or someone else that these people can be expected to trust.

spam: Unsolicited e-mail sent to large numbers of computer users.

spoofing: Making a Web site look like the site of a legitimate business, usually done for criminal purposes such as gathering information that can be used in identity theft.

SSL (Secure Socket Layer): A protocol that allows a computer to communicate securely with another computer by using encrypted data.

Trojan horse: A program that looks legitimate or harmless but performs some illicit or harmful application when it is run, such as capturing passwords or creating an opening through which a hacker may later take control of the computer.

USB (universal serial bus): A hardware interface that allows peripheral devices such as a mouse, scanner, or printer to be connected to a computer.

virus: Hidden software that causes a program to perform some illicit or undesirable action, ranging from posting a prank message to completely destroying a computer's programs and data. A virus may remain dormant until some event, such as a certain date, triggers its activity. It may copy itself into many programs within a single computer or into messages sent to other computers. It may run only once or multiple times.

vulnerability assessment: A systematic examination of a business's computer hardware and software to reveal security vulnerabilities that might allow hackers to enter and damage the computer system.

worm: A program that copies itself over and over in a computer's memory and disk or throughout a network, wasting resources and eventually slowing the system down or causing it to stop functioning (crash).

Y2K bug: A problem predicted to occur in many computers in the year 2000 because dating systems in computers of the time registered only the last two digits of the year and thus were not expected to correctly interpret the new century date. In fact, very few instances of the problem materialized.

Organizations to Contact

The editors have compiled the following list of organizations concerned with the issues debated in this book. The descriptions are derived from materials provided by the organizations. All have publications or information available for interested readers. The list was compiled on the date of publication of the present volume; the information provided here may change. Be aware that many organizations take several weeks or longer to respond to inquiries, so allow as much time as possible.

American Civil Liberties Union (ACLU)
125 Broad St., 18th Fl., New York, NY 10004
(888) 567-2258
Web site: www.aclu.org

The American Civil Liberties Union calls itself "our nation's guardian of liberty." It is usually held to be the foremost civil liberties organization in the United States. It has become involved in litigation and education on a wide variety of issues related to computer crime, including freedom of expression, Internet filtering, and privacy. Its Web site describes current news events, court cases, and legislation pertaining to its issues of interest. It will provide e-mail updates on the issues to members on request.

Anti-Phishing Working Group
e-mail: info@anti-phishing.org • Web site: www.antiphishing.org

The Anti-Phishing Working Group is an association of financial institutions, online retailers, and other businesses formed to fight phishing (sending fraudulent e-mails that attempt to persuade computer users to give out personal information that can be used for identity theft) and spoofing (use of fraudulent Web sites that imitate those of trusted businesses, such as banks or eBay, for the same purpose). The group's Web site reports on trends in phishing attacks, offers an extensive archive of the contents of actual phishing and spoof messages and sites, and includes a form for reporting phishing attacks.

Center for Democracy and Technology (CDT)
1634 I St. NW, Suite 1100, Washington, DC 20006
(202) 637-9800
e-mail: feedback@cdt.org • Web site: www.cdt.org

The Center for Democracy and Technology promotes libertarian values such as free expression and privacy in issues involving the use of the Internet and other information technologies. Its Web site covers the Children's Online Protection Act and other legislation aimed at keeping young people away from content deemed unsuitable for them, spam, spyware, digital authentication, copyright and online piracy, cyberterrorism, and government surveillance. The site includes news breaks and descriptions of and comments on current legislation and court cases.

The Children's Partnership (TCP)
2000 P St. NW, Suite 330, Washington, DC 20036
(202) 429-0033
e-mail: frontdoor@childrenspartnership.org
Web site: www.childrenspartnership.org

This nonprofit, nonpartisan organization provides public policy analysis and advocacy on behalf of children. TCP's Children and Technology program promotes improved Internet access and content for children. The organization's Web site includes a Parents' Online Resource Center and "Parents' Guide to the Information Superhighway."

Computer Crime Research Center
PO Box 8010, Zaporozhye 95, Ukraine 69095
+38 (061) 2621-472
e-mail: ccrc@crime-research.org • Web site: www.crime-research.org

This independent institute "dedicated to the research of cyber crime, cyber terrorism, and other issues of computer crimes and internet fraud phenomena" is part of a program jointly funded by the United States and Ukraine. Its Web site includes articles, news stories, descriptions of relevant legislation, archives, links, and other resources on cybercrime worldwide.

Crimes Against Children Research Center
University of New Hampshire, 20 College Rd.
#126 Horton Social Science Center, Durham, NH 03824
(603) 862-1888
e-mail: Kelly.foster@unh.edu • Web site: www.unh.edu

This university-based center, created in 1998, researches crimes and abuse against children, both conventional and online. Its work includes some of the first comprehensive studies on children's exposure to sexual materials and contacts on the Internet. Recent reports posted on its Web site include *Internet Sex Crimes Against Minors: The Response of Law Enforcement.*

CyberAngels
PO Box 3171, Allentown, PA 18106
(610) 377-2966
e-mail: caexec@cyberangels.org • Web site: www.cyberangels.org

CyberAngels, a program of the Guardian Angels, a well-known crime victim support and advocacy group, attempts to combat Internet-based crimes including cyberstalking, hacking, viruses and worms, and child abuse and child pornography. Founded in 1995, it bills itself as the world's oldest and largest Internet safety organization. The group educates children, parents, and the general public about safe Internet practices and provides resources for persons (both children and adults) who believe they are being stalked, hacked, or otherwise victimized by means of computers.

Electronic Frontier Foundation
454 Shotwell St., San Francisco, CA 94110
(415) 436-9333
e-mail: information@eff.org • Web site: www.eff.org

This organization, often described as "the ACLU of cyberspace," was founded in 1990 in response to an early federal hacker crackdown that threatened free speech by shutting down Web sites that were not involved in crimes. Since then the group has strongly advocated for privacy protection, public access to encryption technologies, and freedom of expression. It opposes Internet censorship or blocking, which is often proposed in the name of protecting children from pornography, and efforts by the recording industry and other copyright holders to overly restrict the fair use of their products. Its Web site covers court cases, legislation, and other news related to the organization's topics of interest and includes extensive links.

Electronic Privacy Information Center (EPIC)
1718 Connecticut Ave. NW, Suite 200, Washington, DC 20009
(202) 483-1140
Web site: www.epic.org

This group, established in 1994, focuses on the need to protect privacy and freedom of expression in the online world, both of which are closely related to cybercrime issues such as spam and e-mail fraud, identity theft, and Internet censorship aimed at protecting copyright holders or shielding children from pornography. The EPIC Web site includes reports and books, tracking of current legislation and court cases, and news stories. EPIC also offers a free newsletter, *EPIC Alert*, and links to related organizations. A separate Web site, www.privacy.org, presents additional news, information, and calls for action.

Federal Bureau of Investigation (FBI)
J. Edgar Hoover Building
935 Pennsylvania Ave. NW, Washington, DC 20535-0001
(202) 324-3000
Web site: www.fbi.gov

The FBI is the chief criminal investigative agency of the U.S. government. Its Cyber Crimes Program handles computer-related offenses such as hacking and system attacks, theft of information, fraud, and online sexual predators. Its Crimes Against Children investigative program and the Innocent Images National Initiative focus on child pornographers. Documents related to these programs can be accessed by typing the name of the program into the search engine on the FBI Web site.

Federal Trade Commission (FTC)
600 Pennsylvania Ave. NW, Washington, DC 20580
(202) 326-2222
Web site: www.ftc.gov

This government agency, founded in 1914, regulates business under federal law. One of its jobs is protecting consumers from misleading advertising, invasion of privacy, and fraud, including identity theft, whether these crimes involve computers or not. Material on identity theft, e-commerce and the Internet, and privacy can be found on the agency's Web site under Consumer Information: For Consumers.

National Cyber Security Partnership (NCSP)
(202) 715-1561
Web site: www.cyberpartnership.org

The NCSP is an alliance of the Business Software Alliance, the Information Technology Association of America, TechNet, and the U.S. Chamber of Commerce in partnership with various government agencies, academics, and industry experts. It calls itself a "public-private partnership to make the Internet more secure." Formed to help in implementing the George W. Bush administration's National Strategy to Secure Cyberspace, the group has five task forces covering awareness for home users and small business, cybersecurity early warning, corporate governance, security across the software development life cycle, and technical standards and common criteria. Each of these task forces prepared a report in early 2004; these reports are available on the group's Web site.

National Fraud Information Center
c/o National Consumers League
1701 K St. NW, Suite 1200, Washington, DC 20006
(202) 835-3323
e-mail: info@nclnet.org • Web site: www.fraud.org

The National Consumers League formed the National Fraud Information Center to educate consumers about telemarketing and Internet fraud. The center's Web site offers tips on common frauds and scams, including Internet fraud, scams against businesses, and counterfeit drugs (which are often sold over the Internet). The site includes an online form for reporting suspected fraud.

SpamCon Foundation
829 Fourteenth St., San Francisco, CA 94114
(415) 552-2557
e-mail: comments@spamcon.org • Web site: http://spamcon.org

This nonprofit organization supports measures to reduce the incidence of unsolicited e-mail (spam), which imposes substantial costs on Internet service providers, reduces workers' productivity, and serves as a conduit for fraud. The Web site provides information about best practices and techniques to help service providers and users avoid spam. It also covers and comments on breaking news, current legislation and court cases, discussions, statistics, and lists of relevant books and periodicals.

U.S. Department of Justice, Criminal Division, Computer Crime and Intellectual Property Division
John C. Keeney Building
Suite 600, Tenth and Constitution Aves. NW, Washington, DC 20530
(202) 514-1026
Web site: www.usdoj.gov

This section of the Department of Justice coordinates and provides resources for federal prosecution of computer crimes. Its Web site offers many resources, including descriptions of policy, cases, guidance, laws, and documents relating to computer crime, intellectual property crime, and computer ethics. Documents available on the site include press releases, speeches, testimony, reports, and manuals. One section of the site is especially for parents, teachers, and students.

U.S. Secret Service
Office of Government Liason and Public Affairs
245 Murray Dr., Bldg. 410, Washington, DC 20223
(202) 406-5708
Web site: www.ustreas.gov

The U.S. Secret Service has historically been involved in the fight against counterfeiting. Today the agency helps to protect computers used in interstate commerce from cyberattacks. The Secret Service also investigates financial fraud, identity theft, and other crimes affecting the nation's financial, banking, and telecommunications infrastructure. The agency's Web site has a section containing the answers to questions frequently asked by students.

Working to Halt Online Abuse
c/o J.A. Hitchcock, PO Box 696, Dover, NH 03821-0696
(561) 828-2801
e-mail: whoa@haltabuse.org • Web site: www.haltabuse.org

This volunteer organization, founded by writer Jayne A. Hitchcock in 1997, seeks "to fight online harassment through education of the general public, education of law enforcement personnel, and empowerment of victims." The group works with people who are being harassed online, educates people about ways to avoid harassment or minimize its effects, and helps online communities develop policies to create a safer social environment. Its Web site includes statistics about cyberstalking and an online safety brochure.

Bibliography

Books

Dan Appleman — *Always Use Protection: A Teen's Guide to Safe Computing.* Berkeley, CA: APress, 2004.

Carlos A. Arnaldo — *Child Abuse on the Internet: Ending the Silence.* New York: Berghahn, 2001.

Steven Branigan — *High-Tech Crimes Revealed.* Indianapolis, IN: Addison-Wesley Professional, 2004.

David Finkelhor, Kimberly J. Mitchell, and Janis Wolak — *Online Victimization: A Report on the Nation's Youth by the Crimes Against Children Research Center.* Alexandria, VA: National Center for Missing and Exploited Children, 2000.

Steven Furnell — *Cybercrime.* Boston: Addison-Wesley Professional, 2001.

Eric Gertler — *Prying Eyes: Protect Your Privacy from People Who Sell to You, Snoop on You, or Steal from You.* New York: Random House Reference, 2004.

Marjorie Heins — *Not in Front of the Children: Indecency, Censorship, and the Innocence of Youth.* New York: Hill & Wang, 2001.

Jayne A. Hitchcock — *Net Crimes & Misdemeanors: Outmaneuvering the Spammers, Swindlers, and Stalkers Who Are Targeting You Online.* Medford, NJ: Information Today, 2002.

Sarah L. Holloway and Gill Valentine — *Cyberkids: Youth Identities and Communities in the On-Line World.* New York: Routledge, 2001.

Philip Jenkins — *Beyond Tolerance: Child Pornography on the Internet.* New York: New York University Press, 2003.

Bryan H. Joyce — *Internet Scams: What to Be Afraid of in Cyberspace.* Pembroke Pines, FL: Net Works, 2002.

M.E. Kabay — *Cyber-Safety for Everyone: From Kids to Elders.* South Barre, VT: Accura, 2002.

Peter Lilley — *Dot.con.* Sterling Page, VA: Kogan Page, 2002.

David A. May and James E. Headley — *Identity Theft.* New York: Peter Lang, 2004.

Anne P. Mintz, ed. — *Web of Deception: Misinformation on the Internet.* Medford, NJ: Information Today, 2002.

Kevin D. Mitnick and William L. Simon
The Art of Deception: Controlling the Human Element of Security. Indianapolis, IN: Wiley, 2002.

Michael Newton
The Encyclopedia of High-Tech Crime and Crime-Fighting. New York: Checkmark, 2004.

Richard Power
Tangled Web: Tales of Digital Crime from the Shadows of Cyberspace. Upper Saddle River, NJ: Pearson Education, 2000.

Kevin F. Rothman
Coping with Dangers on the Internet: A Teen's Guide to Staying Safe Online. New York: Rosen, 2000.

Marcia Smith and Amanda Jacobs
Internet: Status Report on Attempts to Protect Children from Unsuitable Material on the Web. Washington, DC: Congressional Research Service, updated January 28, 2004.

Richard A. Spinello
Regulating Cyberspace: The Policies and Technologies of Control. Westport, CT: Quorum, 2002.

Cliff Stearns, ed.
On-Line Fraud & Crime: Are Consumers Safe? Collingwood, PA: DIANE, 2001.

Bob Sullivan
Your Evil Twin: Behind the Identity Theft Epidemic. New York: Wiley, 2004.

James T. Thomes
Dotcons: Con Games, Fraud & Deceit on the Internet. San Jose, CA: Writers Club Press, 2000.

Dan Verton
The Hacker Diaries: Confessions of Teenage Hackers. Emeryville, CA: McGraw-Hill/Osborne, 2002.

White House
National Strategy to Secure Cyberspace. Washington, DC: White House, 2003. www.us-cert.gov/reading_room/cyberspace_strategy.pdf.

Becky Worley
TechTV's Security Alert: Stories of Real People Protecting Themselves from Identity Theft, Scams, and Viruses. Indianapolis, IN: TechTV/New Riders/Pearson Education, 2004.

Periodicals

Richard Adams
"He May Be a White Hat, a Black Hat, a Phreaker or a Script Kiddie, but Is He Just a Vandal, or Is He a Modern-Day Hero?" *New Statesman*, September 4, 2000.

H.L. Armstrong and P.J. Forde
"Internet Anonymity Practices in Computer Crime," *Information Management & Computer Security*, October 22, 2003.

Pete Barlas
"Anti-Phishing Group Intends to Reel In Online Identity Thieves," *Investor's Business Daily*, March 12, 2004.

Emily Benedek
"Web Attack in the Workplace," *Newsweek*, May 13, 2002.

Maggie Biggs	"Invasion of the Data Snatchers," *Computer User*, May 2003.
Susan W. Brenner	"U.S. Cybercrime Law: Defining Offenses," *Information Systems Frontiers*, June 2004.
Peter A. Buxbaum	"Nine-Digit Dilemma," *Computerworld*, October 13, 2003.
Dan Carney	"Online Scambusters," *Business Week*, April 3, 2000.
Ted Crooks	"Fear of ID Theft May Do More Harm than the Crime," *American Banker*, May 27, 2004.
Karl Cushing	"Private Eyes," *Computer Weekly*, May 23, 2002.
Kristin Davis	"Targeting Kids for Identity Theft," *Kiplinger's Personal Finance*, January 2004.
Robert D'Ovidio and James Doyle	"A Study on Cyberstalking," *FBI Law Enforcement Bulletin*, March 2003.
Sunil Dutta	"Identity Theft: A Crime of Modern Times," *World & I*, October 2003.
Economist	"Unlimited Opportunities?" May 15, 2004.
Julian Fantino	"Child Pornography on the Internet," *Police Chief*, December 2003.
Jerry Finn	"A Survey of Online Harassment at a University Campus," *Journal of Interpersonal Violence*, April 2004.
Ed Foster	"Phony Lotteries, Domain Name Extortion May Be the Latest Internet Con," *InfoWorld*, January 8, 2001.
Kim Gilmour	"In 2001, This Man Was Given Three Years and 15m [pounds] to Combat Organised Crime on the Internet. Two Years Later We Ask Len Hynds If It Was Time and Money Well Spent," *Internet Magazine*, May 2003.
Lea Goldman	"Cybercon," *Forbes*, October 4, 2004.
Reid Goldsborough	"Protecting Yourself Against Viruses, Worms, and Other Humiliation," *Poptronics*, February 2002.
Ghulam Hasnain et al.	"School for Hackers," *Time*, May 22, 2000.
Information Age	"The Social Side of Security," September 10, 2002.
InformationWeek	"Big Bad World," September 1, 2003.
Richard Johnston	"The Battle Against White-Collar Crime," *USA Today*, January 2002.
Hal Karp	"Angels Online," *Reader's Digest*, April 2000.
Scott Kirsner	"Catch Me If You Can," *Fast Company*, August 2003.

Jason Krause	"Can Anyone Stop Internet Porn?" *ABA Journal*, September 2002.
Robert Lenzner and Nathan Vardi	"Cyber-Nightmare," *Forbes Global*, September 20, 2004.
Mark Lewis	"Policing Cyberspace," *Computer Weekly*, April 22, 2003.
Margaret Mannix et al.	"The Internet's Dark Side: Internet Crime," *U.S. News & World Report*, August 28, 2000.
George R. Milne	"How Well Do Consumers Protect Themselves from Identity Theft?" *Journal of Consumer Affairs*, Winter 2003.
Jim Morrison	"Protecting Kids from CyberWolves," *FamilyPC*, April 2001.
Bob Palmer	"Protect Your Kids from Pedophiles by Being Computer Savvy," *Memphis Business Journal*, September 14, 2001.
James F. Pasley	"United States Homeland Security in the Information Age," *White House Studies*, Fall 2003.
David Piscitello and Stephen Kent	"The Sad and Increasingly Deplorable State of Internet Security," *Business Communications Review*, February 2003.
Laura Rich	"Click Here for Revenge," *Cosmopolitan*, May 2000.
Jonathan J. Rusch	"Identity Theft: Fact and Fiction," *C/Net News.com*, September 18, 2002.
Anne Kates Smith and Mark Popowski	"What Were They Thinking?" *Kiplinger's Personal Finance*, April 2002.
B.H. Spitzberg and G. Hobbler	"Cyberstalking and the Technologies of Interpersonal Terrorism," *New Media & Society*, March 2002.
Bill Thompson	"Hackers," *Internet Magazine*, January 15, 2004.
Cristina Vudhiwat	"Developing Threats: Cyberstalking and the Criminal Justice System," *Crime & Justice International*, September 2002.
Stephen H. Wildstrom	"Software Scams on Internet Time," *Business Week*, September 30, 2002.

Index

106